C80502651

# Why Trade It In?

## KEEP YOUR CAR TROUBLE - FREE

**GEORGE AND SUZANNE FREMON**

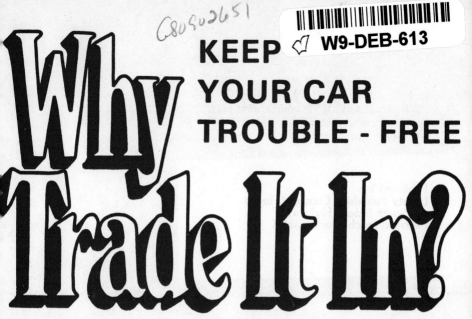

Nov 30, 1983

Dear Prof Bowling,

I wish you the modern travellers blessing:
(without any reference to St. Christopher I'm afraid)

May you own your Pontiac indefinately,
and may it provide you with hundreds
of thousands of safe and pleasant
motoring.   —fondest regards, Vincent

© Suzanne Fremon 1983, 1991
LIBERTY PUBLISHING COMPANY
Deerfield Beach, Florida

Fourth Edition, September 1991

*Distributed by:*

COOL HAND COMMUNICATIONS, INC.
A Publishing Company

Library of Congress #82-84277
ISBN 0-89709-194-9

*To the mechanics we have known and loved:*

   *to Ashton,*
      *and Joe,*
         *and Andy,*
            *and Frank,*
               *and Leo,*
                  *and Angelo,*
                     *and Walt,*
                        *and Bill,*
                           *and Reliable Old Bert,*

      *this book is affectionately dedicated.*

# Contents

# Introduction

If you are looking at this book with serious intent, congratulations! You have never been in better or more numerous company. Millions of your responsible fellow-citizens share your intention: to make their cars last. And their reasons are much the same as yours: either they can't afford a new car (or even a newer car) at all, or they have placed a new car fairly far down on their list of priorities.

You may never in your life have owned a car that was more than five years old—or if you did, you may now regard Life After Five with some dread, remembering that old bucketabolts as a source of constant worry. You couldn't trust it for any serious travel much beyond the city limits; you never knew when it would let you down in an emergency. It kept you on tenterhooks.

So if you are now thinking seriously of making your present car last far longer than you ever tried to do before, you may have some questions: Can I get away with it? And not just barely get away with it, but will I have a car that does what I need it to do? Will keeping it going cost more in repairs than a newer car would cost? Above all, given the fact that I am no mechanic, can I really manage it? How?

Our answers to these questions are emphatic. With a few exceptions, described below, our answers are these:

Can I get away with it? YES. You can have your present car maintained so that it will be as reliable as any new (or newer) car you may be considering. And you can keep it in good shape for several hundred thousand miles if you want to.

Will it cost more in repairs than a newer car would cost? NO. You will not spend more to keep your present car going to your complete satisfaction than you would spend to buy a newer car and keep *it* going (perhaps *not* to your complete satisfaction).

Can *I* really manage this project without being a mechanic myself? YES. A non-mechanic (which after all most people are) can indeed manage the maintaining of a car with the help of a competent mechanic who does the actual work and participates to a reasonable extent in the planning.

The exceptions to our confident answers are these:

1. the "unitized body" (or "unibody") car that has not been adequately protected from rust on the underside;

2. the make and model of a car, domestic or imported, that is known to embody spectacularly bad design innovations, and that should never have been put on the market in the first place; and

3. the ten-year-old (or older) specimen of a not-very-popular make and model, for which it may be difficult to find replacement parts.

Your mechanic can help you appraise your present car if you have any doubts about it: he will inspect the underside for rust, tell you if your model is known among mechanics as flawed from birth, and testify as to how easy or difficult it is to obtain replacement parts.

Most people have serious misgivings about all cars that are older than four or five or six years old. This attitude is part of our legacy from the Golden Age of the Automobile, a period that began in the mid-Twenties and lasted through the Seventies. Car manufacturers had their world well in hand in those years: their only imperative was to sell cars, and this they did superbly well, however badly they did everything else. They persuaded middle-class families that they should routinely replace the family car every two to five years. It is more economical, they said, to replace it than to try to maintain it longer.

This was all nonsense, of course. In the middle Twenties, General Motors invented the concept known as the Annual Model—a gimmick devised solely for the purpose of selling cars. And for as long as the public lapped up this particular snake oil, not many people wondered about the wisdom of scrapping cars that could have served for many years longer. At the time, it looked as though this idiocy would never end.

But it did end. Car owners began *not* visiting dealers' showrooms. They began *not* buying cars. They began putting off the buying of new cars as long as they could.

The simplest explanation of this phenomenon is the most familiar: "I haven't got the money." But there may also be a more profound explanation. People never have the money for *all* the things they want, but most middle-class citizens manage to buy the things they want most. If the public in general believed it was important to buy new cars every two or three or four years, we would still be buying twelve million new cars every year. But we don't: and some of us believe it was never either necessary or desirable to dance to that auto-industry tune.

In today's circumstances, the industry's new-car tune typically starts with your (or our) hypothetical six-year-old medium-sized sedan that shows 65,000 miles on its odometer and gets 20 miles to the gallon in ordinary service. Trade it in on a smaller car, sings the tune, and reduce your gasoline bill by maybe half, and for five years spend less in repairs than you would spend on your present car. Your savings in the first five or six years would pay back all of the cash you spent on the trade-in; and then you would have a six-year-old car with pretty good trade-in value instead of a 12-year-old car with negligible trade-in value. How could you lose?

The proposition is beguiling. If only it were true—which it isn't! In the sales-talk, "the cash you will spend" is the negotiated price of the new car minus your trade-in allowance. No mention of the sales tax on your purchase: several hundred dollars. Or the higher insurance you will carry on the new car, and the higher premiums you will pay. Or the higher cost of repairing a modern high-tech automobile, for as long as you own it: bearings that can't be simply lubricated but instead have to be replaced, and expensive electronic "black boxes" that cannot be repaired and also have to be replaced. And worst of all, no mention of the huge cost of the money you will tie up in the new car, money you will either borrow or withdraw from your money-earning investments or savings account.

So the net cost of the new car will be not simply the difference between the negotiated price and the trade-in allowance for your old car. It is more likely to be *double* that amount; and savings in operating costs will *never* equal the amount you actually pay out to acquire a new car.

This is not to say you should never buy a new or newer car. You will do so, and so will we. But when the time comes to replace the venerable charmer we now drive, we will be under no illusions about the replacement's "paying for itself," or even costing us less, overall, than our present car. For as long as our mechanic can find repair parts for it, our present car costs us less—a lot less—than we would spend for any new or substantially newer car. When we do make a change, it will be because we *want* to do so and are willing to spend the money for it.

A lot of other people appear to have the same attitude about it that we do. As exciting as it is to buy a new car, millions of people are thinking they'll keep the present one going, at least for the time being. They are no longer asking themselves "How long will I have to put up with this old car?" but rather "How long will this car do the job safely and reliably?"

The answer is "Probably for a long, long time."

We hope this book will help you keep your car going for as long as you *want* to keep it going.

# What This Book Is About

This book is about having your car maintained, *without doing any of the work yourself*, so that it will run safely, reliably, and satisfactorily, for as long as you want it to—for 200,000 or 300,000 miles if you wish. It does not tell you how to inspect or lubricate or adjust or repair or replace anything; instead, it tells you *what to have done* and *when to have it done*, and—if you care to know—*why*.

You will need the services of a conscientious mechanic. The more competent your mechanic, the better; but it is not essential that he be a whiz in order to serve your needs if he is honest (a minimum requirement in any case) and articulate enough and interested enough in you so that you can communicate with each other. Finding such a mechanic will not be the easiest job you ever undertook, but neither is it impossible. A chapter called "Your Mechanic and You" begins on page 9; it may be of some help.

Note that the mechanic-and-you chapter is not only about your mechanic. It is also about *YOU*. Nobody would expect a veterinarian to do a good job on a dog, or cat, or horse if the veterinarian had to rely solely on the patient for information about symptoms. He needs someone—the patient's owner—to describe those symptoms. The owner, of course, need not be an expert in pathology to enable the veterinarian to do a good job; but if doctor and patient are to be successful together, it is essential that the veterinarian start with a description of the situation by somebody who knows something about normal behavior, is able to recognize abnormal behavior, and has some knowledge about what a vet can reasonably expect to achieve. "Your Mechanic and You" is therefore about not only the good-mechanic problem, but also the equally important good-customer problem.

What to have done, and when to have it done, constitute a **Maintenance Program.** Suggested **Maintenance Schedules,** which list things to have done at 5,000-mile intervals up to 100,000 miles (when the cycle simply starts over), are presented in the chapter that begins on page 27. Some of the items have to do with lubrication or adjustments, or both, to forestall premature wearing-out; some call for prompt replacement of components at first indication of wear, to avoid accelerated wearing-out of other, more-expensive components; and some maintenance items call for replacing critical components—radiator hoses, batteries, and fuel pumps, for example—well before they are likely to fail, because the consequences of their failing may be so dire that the cost of premature replacing are small by comparison.

You will also need the services of a conscientious body shop. Keeping up with RUST (or preferably keeping ahead of it) is a serious psychological matter for virtually all car owners. For many, it is also a matter of maintaining the structural integrity of the vehicle. (See discussion of "unitized body" on page 18. It is contained in the chapter entitled "Fighting Rust and Other Ailments" which begins on page 17.)

Like the chapter about mechanics, this discussion emphasizes the role that YOU, the owner, must play in the maintenance program. Mechanical deterioration is likely to provide the motivation to get you to a garage if you have neglected maintenance; rust is less likely to do so, since rust is always silent. YOU have to provide the motivation yourself.

A section that begins on page 143 lists a wide array of behavior problems: the noises, shakes, shudders, silences and aromas that are your car's vocabulary for telling you that something is wrong. Some of the ailments will be trivial, some will be serious, and most will be in-between, but you will be wise to take them all seriously.

The final chapter, just before the index, is a Glossary— definitions of automobile terms that are used in too many different connections to permit defining each time they are used. If in the text you encounter a term that is neither defined on the spot nor an item of general knowledge, look it up in the Glossary, and if it is not there, consult a dictionary.

The remainder of the book is devoted to descriptions of the workings of your car. This section is not intended to be read at one sitting, but rather to be consulted as your needs and your curiosity dictate. An automobile is an ingenious machine, made up of hundreds of simple parts, organized into systems (the fuel system, the brake system, and so on) that fit neatly and work smoothly together to form an operating vehicle. To one who does not comprehend it, an automobile can be intimidating; but to one who does understand it, it can be a thing of elegant beauty and deep satisfaction. The understanding is not difficult. The whole is complex, but the individual parts are not, and the systems they form are logical. You will grasp it all eventually, if you want to; just take it piece by piece, and remember that there is no hurry. You have the rest of your life to learn about automobiles. Meanwhile, step by step you can achieve the satisfaction of knowing enough to not be helpless.

# Your Mechanic and You

We were not just being jocular when we dedicated this book to "mechanics we have known and loved" over the past 40 years. A competent, conscientious mechanic and—just as important—a good working relationship between mechanic and car owner are essential to achieving your aim: to keep your car in satisfactory service year after year after year.

The most useful mechanic for you will be someone who has been in the business long enough to have had a lot of experience, so you might think of 35 as a minimum age.

Your ideal mechanic will of course be honest. Initially, you'll have to judge his honesty by a combination of his reputation and your own first impressions. After you've worked with him for a while, you'll know more about his honesty from your own experience.

One key to a mechanic's experience, judgment, and probable competence and honesty, is his immediate response when you take your car to him with an ailment. Some car problems are simple and can be diagnosed quickly, but most are not, and a wise and reliable mechanic knows this and knows how easy it is to chase the wrong cause. A mechanic who tells you in a flash, whenever you take a problem to him, exactly what's the matter with your car before he has a chance to study it, is a mechanic you can do without; he'll be wrong as often as not.

The ideal mechanic will be conscientious about scheduling jobs, and when he tells you your car will be ready on Tuesday afternoon, it will be ready. Not always, because he has emergencies in his life like everyone else, and you have to accept that; but almost always.

He will be a person you can talk to, and who will be willing to talk to you. You and he will be embarking on a mutual educational experience; you will be learning about technical matters from him, and he will be learning from you what you want from your car and what your priorities are. You must feel able to say, for example, that you don't have a lot of money and you need to be careful. On the other hand, you may want him to do some things that he may consider unnecessary, like replacing a part before it has worn out. You must be able to discuss these things with him. In short, you need someone you have confidence in and feel comfortable with.

If you are female, you may have the special problems of a woman in a world that often seems oppressively male. Many mechanics treat women either as hopeless idiots or as scatterbrains, cute but dumb. These attitudes can be irritating, but they shouldn't necessarily wash out a mechanic as a possibility. If he is good in other respects, he may even be able to learn from you that some women are serious about their cars, and deserve to be taken seriously. He may even come to look on you as his special student, and you may find out later that he has been bragging about you—which you may not like any better than his previous view of you. In any case, whatever his attitude, yours should show clearly that although you may not know a lot about cars, you are learning and plan to continue learning. And while you learn you might tell yourself a little-recognized fact: that most men don't know very much about cars either.

The service station where you normally buy gas may be able to do minor repair work as well as a full-service garage. You may have been buying gasoline all along at a full-service garage that doubles as a filling station; but even failing that, your service station may be able to do routine lubrications and routine ignition- and brake-system maintenance—and be a lot more convenient for you than the nearest full-service garage.

Beware, however, of any service station or small garage where the owner or manager doesn't do any of the repair work himself, because he has "a mechanic in the shop who really knows his stuff." We wouldn't count on anybody in the shop being a better mechanic than the boss. Beware too of the service-station or small-garage owner or manager who is too busy to talk to you about your car. It will probably turn out that he has more things going on than he can handle properly, and your car shouldn't be in a shop where the boss can't take care of his business.

You would do well to investigate the service department of the official dealer for your make of car. It almost certainly maintains the largest local stock of repair parts for your model, has any specialized tools needed for working on it, and receives a continuous stream of service bulletins about unusual problems with your model that experience has brought to light. During the Golden Age of the Automobile, dealers tended to neglect (or even, it sometimes seemed, actively discourage) maintenance and repair services and concentrate almost totally on the selling of new cars. This may still be true of some official new-car dealers, but the Great Automobile Depression of the early-Eighties caused many dealers to become very serious about their maintenance-and-repair services. Another mark against dealers' shops during the Golden Age was their high prices compared with free-lance shops. Again, this may still be true in your neighborhood, but not necessarily. The demand for competent mechanics is very high and increasing, and many free-lance garages have necessarily become top-dollar shops too. In addition, the flood of automobile innovations in recent years has made it harder and harder for work-on-anything shops to keep up. If a shop lacks a specialized tool or piece of testing equipment, or is not yet fully familiar with a new component on a car of brand-new vintage, it may have to spend more time on a specific repair job than a better-situated shop would have to spend; and the extra time may well be at your extra expense. The older your car, the less likely is the free-lance shop to suffer this kind of disadvantage; but even so, manufacturers' service bulletins are sometimes addressed to problems in cars that are several models back and that have baffled mechanics for years.

Like most choices having to do with garages, the independent-vs.-dealer question depends on the specific case. Good independent garages have kept up with the times for years, and have matched and often surpassed dealers' shops in knowledge and quality of work. The way to bet is that the good ones will continue to compete successfully on all counts. If you have no prior experience to guide you when you start your search for a mechanic, however, you would probably do well to try the dealer's service department first.

Before discussing further the mechanic half of the mechanic-and-you team, we should give some attention to the other half: you. A garage, like any business, must have an adequate supply of good customers in order to survive; but in today's world, a good garage has less need of another customer than you have for a good garage. In short, you probably need a good mechanic more than he needs you. So while you look for a mechanic you can do business with, you will also serve your own interests by being as easy to do business with as you can.

Any mechanic, however competent and conscientious, may flub a job if he doesn't receive an informative description of the car's symptoms. "It clunks" or "feels like the wheels are about to come off" are not very informative. Better would be: "The engine jerks when I accelerate," "I hear a whine in the back when I turn a corner to the left," or "something up front goes clack-clack when I go over a rough road." Such reports are specific, they give some indication of the location of the problem, the condition under which it occurs, and perhaps (to a knowledgeable listener) the nature of the problem. Combinations of symptoms are often even more informative than individual symptoms; so if the car has manifested abnormal sounds or behavior in addition to the one that has been most worrisome, you should mention the additional symptoms too.

You should never assume that a mechanic will do anything about your car that you do not request very specifically, and you should never assume that a request to "check everything over" is a specific instruction. A mechanic must charge you for time he spends in your service, and his time is expensive. He knows he will probably lose you as a customer if you conclude that he is too expensive—which you would do if he spent hours looking for things that might possibly be wrong. So if something goes wrong with your car shortly after you have had a mechanic work on something else, don't assume the second misfortune is somehow the mechanic's fault.

It takes a long time and serious effort to develop a satisfactory relationship with a mechanic. Much of the effort will be expended in learning how to communicate with each other, and this may mean some misunderstandings at first. He will work for you most effectively after he comes to know you—your prejudices and your predilections. Are you likely, for example, to value time and convenience more than money? This will be important when he is wondering whether you will prefer that he make a repair the expensive way in order to be *sure* of curing an ailment, or do it less expensively knowing that you *might* have to bring the car back a second time. It is also important, when he is in the middle of a repair, that he know pretty confidently whether you will endorse his doing something he finds is needed but that you didn't specifically request.

Once you have identified your mechanic, or at least have made a tentative choice, you will have to give serious thought to the question of buying all of your services and supplies from him. Chain stores of various kinds compete for specialized, high-volume, high-profit automotive business, and—particularly if you take advantage of "advertised specials"—you can often buy tires, batteries, shock absorbers, muffler systems, front-end alignments, tune-ups, brake-system overhauls, and other items and services at prices no full-service garage is able to meet. Just how much you could actually save by doing business with these shops is a local matter, not subject to broad generalizations. In actual practice you would not save as much as the "specials" advertisements indicate. If your brakes are worrying you, you are not likely to live with what might be a dangerous situation until somebody advertises a "brake special" in the newspaper; and in addition, you may not need a brake-overhaul at all—as your own mechanic would tell you, but the specialty shop may not. Similarly, you are likely to have repairs made to the exhaust system when noise or underside inspection shows repairs to be needed, not when an advertisement appears. As a workaday matter, some specialty shops in your area may offer substantially lower prices than full-service garages, but on the other hand the difference may not be great enough to justify your sacrificing the continuity of knowledge and attention you would receive from your own garage.

Your buying practices will of course affect your relationship with the garage you have taken such pains to find. In our long past we have known two favorite garages that "didn't want to fool with" tires and batteries, and actually referred us to chain stores for these items. But this is not the usual posture: goods and services that are high-profit for the retail chains are high-profit for the general garage too. Only you can weigh the apparent attitude of your own garage against your own imperative to find bargains.

**Preventive Maintenance** is a subject you will want to go into rather extensively with your mechanic. Throughout this book you will find recommendations to replace components of your car after periods of service that are obviously arbitrarily selected: radiator hoses after 25,000 miles, for example, fuel pumps after 50,000 miles, and so on. These recommendations are based upon our own observations over the years and reflect our best judgment as to probable average life-expectancies of specific components. They also reflect our belief that sacrificing some part of the remaining life-expectancy of a critical component can be written off as low-cost insurance. (Having to be towed in for repairs is inconvenient, time-consuming, and usually very expensive.)

Do not be shaken, however, if your favorite mechanic is less
enthusiastic than we about preventive maintenance, or if he urges
different replacement intervals than we for making replacements.
Most mechanics have grown up in a world of **corrective
maintenance;** repairing and replacing parts that have failed, but
not replacing serviceable parts, simply on the supposition that
they are likely to fail in some unspecified near future. Some
mechanics regard such anxieties as foolish. Inspect belts and hoses,
yes, and replace them if they appear questionable; but why believe
you can predict how long a belt or a hose or some other component is going to last?

You won't be able to settle on a working philosophy in the
course of a single session on the subject. This is something you
will have to develop over the course of many sessions. This should
not be surprising, because the mechanic's perspective is different
from yours. To him, a burst radiator hose is a simple matter:
he sends his tow truck out, brings the car in to the shop, and
then simply replaces the hose; the customer picks up the car when
it is ready. To you, however, the same burst hose means, at best,
a disruption in your day, and it may be something a lot worse
than a mere disruption: a disabled car on a roaring superhighway
or even in the heart of deserted downtown on Easter Sunday on
your way to Grandma's. To you, it is money well spent to do
anything within reason to avoid breakdowns on the road; to the
mechanic, though, it is risky to make any repair that a customer
might believe, rightly or wrongly, was not needed—he knows
this from his own experience. The whole concept of preventive
maintenance is something you will have to work out between
you, taking plenty of time to do it. No general philosophical formula is likely to fit your specific case precisely.

So you will gradually develop areas of agreement with your
mechanic regarding the philosophy of preventive maintenance.
You will also want to draw on his knowledge and experience in
the matter of life-expectancies of individual components. Our

generalized recommendations cannot take into account specific makes and models of car, or specific climates, or specific combinations of superhighway, city-traffic, suburban, and country-road service. Your mechanic's ideas regarding replacements in your circumstances will be helpful.

In recent decades, investigative reporters and consumer protection experts have pumped a lot of poison into the relationship between car owners and garages. "Garages are robbing you blind" is one gleeful message we are all familiar with by now. Investigative reporters and consumer-protection officials have to earn a living too, but the methods some have used to entrap mechanics are a lot more dishonest than the behavior they have contrived to expose. There are indeed dishonest mechanics and garage owners, just as there are dishonest practitioners in every field. But even so, you will be the loser if you allow blind suspiciousness to dominate your dealings with conscientious, self-respecting mechanics.

Having begun this chapter by referring to "the mechanics we have known and loved," we will conclude it by identifying the mechanic named last in our list on the dedication page: Reliable Old Bert. R. O. Bert personifies our favorite mechanic at any given time, the man—perhaps at some time in the future, but not yet, the woman—in whom we repose our confidence and our hope for easiest solutions to the problems and irritations that Henry Ford bequeathed to an eager world. Over the years, a succession of mechanics have played the role of Reliable Old Bert in our lives. We have moved from town to town; favorite mechanics have retired and favorite mechanics have prospered too well for their own good—whereupon, each time, we have embarked once again on a search for a new Reliable Old Bert. Each incumbent has embodied the mixture of knowledge, experience, conscientiousness, skepticism, wisdom, and patience that we think is right for us. *You* might not like him at all—and he might not really take to you, either.

But with patience and perseverance and luck, you will find your own Reliable Old Bert.

# Fighting Rust And Other Ailments

For most of us, making a car last involves appearance as well as mechanical excellence. If money is so tight that you must choose between them, then of course mechanical maintenance must be given precedence. But—no question about it—the appearance of a car makes a significant difference in the state of mind of most car owners, and—also no question about it—state of mind is important to all of us. It would be hard to prove that a car actually runs better when it is clean and shiny and free of dents and rust, but you wouldn't have to prove it to most car owners; they already know it is true. So if you can afford both mechanical excellence and excellence in appearance, you should by all means have both. You want to make your car last, and no single factor is more important in making it last than your state of mind. If you're proud of the way it looks you'll keep it a lot longer than if you're ashamed of it.

To maintain mechanical excellence you need a good garage, a Reliable Old Bert. To keep up appearances—and therefore morale—you will need a body shop, or perhaps two or three to choose among. (More about this later.) You will also need a firm resolve to consult your body shop *regularly*, at about annual intervals. **Preventive inspection** is the key to preventive maintenance in this aspect of owner morale.

You go about finding a satisfactory body shop in the same way you search for a satisfactory mechanic: by first asking people you know (especially your accident-prone friends!), consulting the yellow pages, and so on, and then getting acquainted with several body shop proprietors or managers.

You will have to choose on the basis of how each one acts and sounds. And as in the case of choosing a mechanic, it is sensible to have the jobs done one at a time, at first, so that you can see how a shop performs on Job A before contracting for Job B and Job C. You may be able to save some money by having everything done at once, but you may find, on the other hand, that while Body Shop X quoted a higher price than Shop Y on Job A, the positions may be reversed in the case of Job B; and on Job C, Shop Z may be less expensive than either.

Body work is much less standardized than mechanical work, and the cost of a given repair may depend to a great extent on the particular talents of a specific worker. Also, it is reasonable to presume that Shop X's quotation on a given job may depend not only on the cost of doing it, but also on the amount and kind of business the shop has in its backlog. So be prepared to search out two or three. Shop-hopping is less serious than it is in the case of mechanics, who can serve you better if they know something about your car's history. With bodyworkers, this factor is much less important.

**The Unitized Body Challenge.** Since the early Sixties, many cars have been built with so-called "unitized bodies"—meaning that the vehicle depends for its structural integrity not on an independent **frame** built of heavy steel (and including crossbraces to assure strength and rigidity), but instead on the light sheet metal from which the body is built.

*It is extremely important to know whether your car has a unitized body* because, if it does, the combating of rust on the underside is very much more important than it is if yours has an honest, old-fashioned frame: sheet metal is much more susceptible to rusting-through than is heavy structural steel.

If your car has a unitized body, and is more than three years old, and you haven't had the under-side inspected within the past six months, you should have a body shop inspect it promptly. If you don't know how your car is constructed, any mechanic can tell you by putting it up on a lift and looking at the underside. We suggest you find out specifically whether it has a full frame or a unitized body.

The unitized body is discussed further on in this chapter, in the section on "Combating Rust."

**Rustproofing.** Rustproofing specialists routinely guarantee rustproofing treatments on new cars for periods of three to five years, and some of the most solidly established companies now guarantee their work (if you will bring the car in annually for free inspection and touch-up) for as long as you own the car.

If your car is not new but seems to be fairly free of rust, you would be wise to consult two or three professional rustproofers about the feasibility of giving it a treatment. You are not likely to be given a guarantee on the work unless competition in your area is intense; but, warranty or not, the primary question is whether rustproofing will significantly retard rusting, and the opinion of a conscientious professional deserves careful consideration.

"Rustproofing" is a term that covers a wide range of operations. It is therefore possible for two people to have quite different things in mind when they discuss it. The simplest operation is to apply a rustproofing coating to surfaces that are easily accessible—floor, frame, gasoline tank, underside of fenders, wheel-wells, the inside floor of the trunk and of the passenger compartment, the well the spare tire rides in, the battery tray, the splash shields under the hood, and inboard of the bumpers, and so on. A less simple operation involves loosening the fenders from the body so that the coating can get into the joints. The most difficult operation is spraying the insides of doors and body panels. This often requires that exterior lights be removed to permit access for the spray wand, or that holes be drilled, and later closed with rubber plugs, in the facings of doors and door openings in the body.

All these surfaces must be cleaned thoroughly before applying the coating. Steam-cleaning is done wherever feasible, but kerosene or some other degreasing cleaner must be used inside the passenger compartment, for example.

In discussing with a rustproofer what should be done for your car, be prepared to settle for less than everything. The professional may advise against treating the insides of doors and panels, for example, because of the amount of rust or dirt already there, but be pretty confident about the areas on the under-side of the car. Or perhaps you may not be able to spend what it would cost to do a complete job, even if it is possible to do it. Don't let that discourage you. Do what you can, and above all, don't steer away from doing as much as you can, simply because you can't do everything.

**Combating Rust.** The first rule is: Start Immediately! The second rule is: Never let up!

Whether or not you rustproof your car, your most useful agent for avoiding rust is **water**—*squirted upward from below.* Your worst enemy is salt, and other enemies are other corrosive chemicals that foul all roads and streets. A mixture of mud and corrosive chemicals, caked firmly and moistly in the frame, in cracks between the fenders and the body, and behind braces that support fenders or bumpers, nibbles away at your car and your pocketbook night and day, every day, winter and summer. If you do your own car washing, by all means wash the parts of the body that are visible, so the car will look pretty, but spend *much more time* washing the under-side, and digging out caked mud wherever you can find it. Look particularly in the drain holes on the under-sides of doors and body panels. These must be kept open, to discourage rusting inside.

If you take your car to a commercial car-washing place, be sure it does a good job of washing the under-side of your car. If it doesn't, you would be well-advised to find a shop that *will* do a good job.

Frequent waxing of the body and the fenders up to a height of two feet or so from the ground is also worthwhile. This is the primary rust belt, subjected constantly to splashing and chemical attack and what amounts to sand-blasting. It needs all the protection you can give it.

If you are not able to find a satisfactory car-wash establishment, your mechanic or your body shop may be able to make suggestions. Failing success along any of these lines, consider recruiting a high-school student from your local youth employment service, if there is one, or even advertising for someone to take over the washing/waxing job. Monthly under-side washing and lower-body waxing would almost certainly save you as much in body-maintenance costs as you would spend for these services.

If serious under-side rusting has already occurred by the time you catch up with it, or if it should occur in the future in spite of your best endeavors, you should have the situation thoroughly appraised before making further substantial expenditures on the car. You will probably be able to have matters set right at a cost that is within reason, but obviously it will be better to be sure. Full frames can be reinforced with structural steel, even if they are quite seriously rusted, and the cost is usually modest. Structural repairs on unitized-body cars are likely to be more expensive, but not likely to be out of the question even though the deterioration is very advanced. If you do have to make repairs to the floorpan of a unitized-body car, you would be well-advised to consult with a professional rustproofer beforehand, to see what kind of rustproofing of the repair zone would be advisable.

Flooring in the passenger compartment and the trunk can ordinarily be replaced at modest cost, even if it is necessary to remove the gasoline tank to weld patches on the trunk floor.

Very small rust spots usually make themselves known by causing brown spots to appear on the car finish. Further rusting may occur rapidly or slowly, depending upon the local cause— depending most particularly on whether water or mud is trapped behind the sheet metal, or whether (a less serious matter) the rust spots merely mark flaws in the paint. Brown spots should be inspected by your body shop promptly, to halt the rusting and limit the damage as much as possible.

If the vinyl roof on your "hardtop convertible" develops lumps or bubbles, it is almost certain that the steel roof underneath has developed sizable rust spots. Such damage should be repaired without delay. A new plastic roof cover can be installed if you wish; but if you don't mind violating the conceit of the automobile stylist who foisted the vinyl covering off on you in the first place, you can simply have the repaired steel roof painted—at much lower cost, and you may like the appearance better.

The second rule for combating rust—Never Let Up!—deserves reiteration. We cannot urge you too strongly to let the calendar rather than your own observation guide you in this never-ending battle. You should take your car to your body shop once a year, faithfully, to see whether you are losing the battle.

The Rusty Bumper poses a singular problem because chromium plating cannot be applied by spraying or brushing, and you can't just side-step the problem by painting the bumper because paint won't stick to chromium plating. Bumpers can be re-plated at moderate cost; but if new bumpers are still available for your car, it may be less expensive to replace than to re-plate.

**Dents, Crumples, and Major Bashes.** The other guy bashes in your rear bumper and trunk, but the trunk will still open and close; and the other guy's insurance company pays you in cash what a body shop would charge to repair the damage, and it's a lot of cash that would come in handy for numerous other things that have nothing to do with rear bumpers or trunks. The car still runs fine; and the bashed-in rear end doesn't put you under the kind of pressure that visible rust exerts: the vision of steel-consuming termites at work, unremittingly gnawing away at your valuable property.

As you struggle with the problem of leaving it vs. repairing it, don't lose sight of your own aesthetic values and their effect on your emotions. If you want to make your car last and last, it is essential to keep up with a multitude of maintenance requirements. What will be the effect on you of trying to live with an unsightly vehicle? Only you can judge; we can only point out that more may be at stake than an unsightly surface blemish.

Most dents and crumples can be corrected by skilled hammering, often followed by coating the surface with a layer of lead and smoothing it to reestablish the original contour. It is sometimes less expensive to replace a battered section of sheet metal, by cutting out the damaged area and welding a piece of new steel sheet into place, than to repair it. It is often less costly to replace rather than repair a fender or trunk lid or outer skin of a door or other body panel. Such replacement parts must ordinarily be ordered from a supplier, and this takes time. Arrangements for body work should be made well in advance.

Folk wisdom tells us that if a car has been in a serious accident, you should junk it: you can't ever make it right again. This is nonsense. Repair shops cope all the time with bent frames, smashed doors, buckled hoods, and crumpled radiators and air-conditioning units. The horror must be horrible indeed to be beyond the restorative powers of a good body shop.

But the myth of unrepairable damage serves the insurance companies well. If "everybody knows" that a severely damaged car cannot be put right again, then if you suffer loss you will probably settle for less than it would cost to restore your car to its previous condition. The practice of declaring a car "totaled," and settling the claim by paying the "book value" of a car of your make and model, is probably the proudest achievement of the automobile-insurance industry. Book value purports to be the average price charged by dealers and established at auctions throughout the United States for the make and model under consideration, as recorded by the National Automobile Dealers Association. This can hardly be considered a good beginning for a cash transaction involving your damaged car. The published numbers reflect the reports of used-car dealers. They also reflect the public perceptions of the worthlessness of used cars— perceptions that have been nurtured for generations by the automobile industry. And finally, they reflect the state of maintenance of the average used car. So if your car has been maintained even moderately well, you will not be able to come anywhere near replacing it at the "blue-book" settlement you receive from the genial insurance adjuster.

State laws vary widely with respect to blue-book settlements for damaged cars. If your car has not been well cared for, the blue-book adjustment would probably not be unfair, but if you have maintained it with a view to the long term, then it would not be fair at all. Whatever the local laws and practices in your state, you are not likely to be barred from small-claims (or even larger-claims) court; and if you have the kind of maintenance records every serious-minded car owner should keep, then the insurance company would probably prefer to award you a fair settlement than defend itself in court. At minimum, you should receive enough to buy a car of your make and model—the blue-book value—plus the additional few hundreds of dollars that would be required to bring an average specimen up to the condition of your own car. Your mechanic and your bodyshop man can help you in establishing a fair demand.

If you should have the misfortune of, for example, wrapping your car around a tree at your own expense, the particulars of having it repaired would in this case too be worth investigating carefully. Again, the book-value of the car has little relevance; the question is how much would you have to spend to acquire a car as satisfactory, and in as good condition, as the one you are thinking to have repaired.

**Exterior trim.** You will almost certainly suffer mishap to a chrome strip or two or three, over the years. Generally speaking, precise replacements are available for the first 10 years; after that, replacement is more difficult, but not impossible. The precise item for your car may not be available, but any competent body shop can provide acceptable alternatives. If worse comes to worst, the shop can remove all signs of the original trim strips and the fixtures they were fastened to, fill up the holes, and provide a smooth shiny surface with no memory of trim at all. This is often an improvement.

**A Complete Paint Job** can work wonders in the appearance of an automobile and the spirits of its owner. This should not be surprising, since we paint houses and boats and furniture in the expectation that new paint will brighten our lives. The same is true of your automobile. The cost of repainting a car varies widely from shop to shop, and so does the quality of the work. It is possible to have high-quality repainting done at modest cost, and it will indeed brighten your attitude toward the car you hope to keep in service.

Automobile manufacturers publish their paint formulas, and matching paint can be provided by any body shop for many years after a given car was produced. The paint formula used on your own car is recorded on an information tag that is permanently affixed to the car. If you have it repainted, the simplest thing is to use the same formula. If you switch to another color, be sure to use a standard car-manufacturer's formula, and **be sure to record** the formula identification number in a safe place, where you will be able to find it. This formula will be urgently needed if you ever have to have a body repair made.

**Interior Lights.** Instrument lights, dome lights, trunk lights, map lights, under-hood lights, and the like are replaceable at modest cost. When they go out, as they will, replace them promptly. They are a convenience and it's foolish to do without them when you can have them so readily.

**Windows and Doors.** The windshield may leak around the edges; the door may drag on something when you open it; the window may rattle; you may have to slam the door harder than you used to; the wind may whistle through the weatherstripping.

All of these can be repaired easily and at moderate cost. Glass replacement is routine, window and windshield gaskets are replaceable, as are the window mechanism and the felt channel the window rides in. Power windows almost never balk, but if they do, all parts can be replaced with advance warning to the body shop to give them time to order. Door clearance and drag are adjustable; no need even to install new parts. Minor repairs usually restore to good health hinges and the swing-check devices that hold doors open, but even if total replacement is needed, they don't cost much.

Windshield and window leaks should be repaired promptly. A rusted spot in the windshield or window opening will have to be repaired before a tight joint can be restored. Even worse is the corrosion that results from a wet carpet, which is where the water will end up if it drips down. It is more costly to replace a floor than a windshield or window seal.

**Upholstery and Carpeting.** Automobile slip covers range from sleazy to superb, with sidelines into garish and gaudy. But without risking bankruptcy, you can buy seat covers that will last from two to six times as long as the original upholstery. Carpeting, too, is available, and even the interior ceiling (it's called the "headliner") and the upholstery on the insides of the doors ("interior door panels") can be replaced at moderate cost.

**Interior Moving Parts.** The primary enemy of heater blowers, air-conditioner units, adjustable seats, radios, ashtrays, cigar lighters, glove compartment doors, and knobs of all kinds is the tendency of owners to be philosophical about their misbehavior or disappearance. By all means be stoic if it pleases you; but you don't have to put up with any of these adversities if they irritate you. The heater blower probably has a worn-out switch or blown fuse. The air conditioner may need a charge of refrigerant or perhaps a new expansion-valve diaphragm. The driver's seat may become difficult to move as the car gets on in years, but your service-station people can clean the tracks and squirt lubricant into the works and put it all back in smooth service quickly. Power seats, like power windows, are ruggedly built and not likely to fail; but if yours do, they can be restored with replacement parts.

**The Aesthetic Imperative.** The maintenance chores considered in this chapter, like most mechanical maintenance chores discussed throughout this book, require more effort to arrange for than to ignore. Unlike most of the mechanical-maintenance chores, however, the chores required for maintaining your car's appearance can for the most part be ignored without inviting immediate dire consequences.

But this is not to say there are no consequences. Automobiles are important in our daily lives, and it is important to most of us that our automobiles give us pleasure, and that we avoid as far as possible the exasperation and depression that a shabby car engenders. An automobile can be a pleasure whatever its age if you want it to be. If it is maintained in good condition, your car can be even more of a pleasure when it is 15 years old than when it is only four.

# Maintenance Schedules

The nine lists on the following pages are the heart of a preventive maintenance program. The first is a list of simple—but by no means unimportant—things to have done at your first gasoline stop each month. (These will require no more than 15 minutes, and usually nearer 10.) The eight lists that follow are organized according to the intervals at which inspections, adjustments, repairs, or replacements should be carried out: some at 5,000-mile intervals, others every 10,000 miles, still others at intervals of 15,000, 25,000, 30,000, 50,000, 75,000, and finally 100,000 miles. If you drive your car about 10,000 miles a year, which is approximately the present-day average, a session with your Reliable Old Bert at intervals of about six months will take care of most of your car-maintenance needs.

Before adopting this maintenance program, however, look up the mileage intervals recommended by the owner's manual for your car for the items listed below. Alongside each item is the maintenance list that includes it.

Change engine oil (5,000-mile list)
Change engine oil filter (10,000-mile list)
Lubricate wheel bearings (25,000-mile list)
Service automatic transmission (25,000-mile list)
Change manual-transmission oil (100,000-mile list)
Drain and refill differential (100,000-mile list)

(In some cars, a *transaxle unit* combines the transmission and differential.) Note on the appropriate maintenance list any discrepancies you find between the mileage intervals recommended by our lists and your owner's manual, respectively. Then consider whether to depart from the maintenance program detailed in the nine maintenance lists. The following comments may be helpful; and, in addition, you may wish to consult with Reliable Old Bert.

Diesel-engine cars and front-wheel-drive cars are comparatively new commercial products, and wisdom as to proper maintenance is still being accumulated. By 1970, American cars had become pretty generally standardized, and one could generalize with confidence about taking care of them. Such generalizations cannot be confidently applied to cars of radically new design, however, with respect to those maintenance steps that the manufacturer says must be taken *more frequently* then general experience dictates. The maintenance program we recommend in this book is relatively conscientious. Most discrepancies you find between our program and the owner's-manual program will be in the direction of *longer* maintenance intervals than we recommend. If the manufacturer recommends *shorter* intervals than we, you would be prudent to observe the shorter intervals—even realizing that experience may demonstrate that the manufacturer, in his uncertainty, leaned over backwards to be safe.

Almost every maintenance operation offers a trade-off between the cost of lubricating and the cost of replacing. You can prolong the life of a joint in the steering system, for example, by having it lubricated very frequently; but if you overdo this preventive measure, you will waste more money on too-frequent lubrication than you would waste by more frequent replacing of the joint.

As a general, practical matter, the most important rule is to follow *a regular schedule* in accordance with reasonable maintenance intervals. Your car's greatest enemy is its owner's tendency to Put It Off. The most important thing is not the precise mileage at which you have a component lubricated, but rather having it lubricated at all, regularly and with reasonable frequency.

Any maintenance schedule proposed for general use is almost certainly less than ideal for your own car. The automobile that is used almost exclusively for trips to the shopping center five miles away three times a week would ideally receive different maintenance treatment from the car that takes its owner to work every day, 50 miles each way on a superhighway. The "best" maintenance schedule would probably not be ideal for any given car; "reasonably acceptable" is about the best you can reasonably hope for.

The owner's manual that came with your car is the most authoritative guide for that car, and no one, including yourself, should reproach you for following it. But even this most authoritative document reflects not only the wisdom of the engineers, but also the clout of the marketing people in the manufacturing firm. So if the owner's manual tells you to change the oil filter only every 15,000 miles, this may represent the best judgment of the engineers, but not necessarily. "Easy maintenance" makes cars easier to sell; and so 15,000-mile intervals may be what the sales people persuaded the engineers to settle for—not what the engineers thought was best.

Our main point in all of this is that there are no absolutes in car maintenance rules. We do believe that intervals shorter than the ones recommended in our maintenance schedules should be observed if your owner's manual prescribes them; and if the intervals in the manual are longer than those in the maintenance schedules, observe the longer intervals if they suit your convenience. But whatever schedule you decide upon, you would be wise to follow it pretty carefully.

If your car is a new one, you should follow the maintenance schedule in the owner's manual faithfully, throughout the warranty period, and then consider how you want to proceed after that.

If your car is not new when you embark upon a comprehensive preventive-maintenance program, then your first step will be to have it brought up to good mechanical condition. Thus, for example, if the odometer shows 40,000 miles, you should have everything done that is listed in the "first-of-the-month" list and in the 5,000-mile, 10,000-mile, 15,000-mile, and 25,000-mile lists, excluding only those things that you know have been done within the mileage interval covered by applicable list, and *when* each one was done. Your garage shop tickets may enable you to defer some of the prescribed maintenance operations because they are not yet due again; but lacking specific information, you will be well-advised to have all of the things done that the lists show to be needed to bring your car up-to-date. Thereafter, keeping up your program of preventive maintenance is simply a matter of having the things done that the maintenance lists tell you to have done.

You may be hesitant about handing a mechanic a long list of things to do, when you take your car in for service. You may be accustomed to simply leaving the car for "whatever has to be done," and a little bit timid about specifying things you don't feel you completely understand—and for all you know, the mechanic may already do some of those things routinely, and will only be offended if you explicitly specify them.

You can't have it both ways—on the one hand being an agreeable ignoramus, and, on the other, asking the mechanic to please clean the connection between the engine and the negative battery cable—but you can certainly work into a new relationship with your mechanic by comfortable stages. There is nothing dishonorable about wanting to keep your car going into the infinite (or at least the unlimited) future, and nothing dishonorable about owning a book that suggests specific things to do to make this possible. Reliable Old Bert—the R. O. Bert you already know or the one you will find—will welcome specific authorization to do things that will keep your car in good condition and that he will get paid to do. He will also welcome *being consulted* about what ought to be done—within reason, and not too extensively, especially at his rush hour when he must deal with a whole parade of customers. You may have to find out from Bert what equipment your car has: fuel-injection or carburetor?; electronic ignition or breaker-point ignition?; a catalytic converter?; an air-injection reactor?; and so on. You may want to offer him your copy of this book, for his inspection. Generally speaking, mechanics of yesteryear had a low opinion of books, but this is changing slowly.

The most likely adverse reaction on R. O. Bert's part will have to do with things that "there's no sense in." There is no need for confrontation. Any disagreement will probably have to do with this or that preventive-maintenance item, and it will probably come down to a question of Bert's opinion as to *when* the preventive step should be taken, not whether—and your chances of being stranded by the side of the road if you and he guess wrong.

So you will feel your way long. If your mechanic is the Reliable Old Bert you want, together you will develop a maintenance program for your car that will keep it going satisfactorily—and pleasurably—for as long as you want it to go.

It is important to **keep a record** of everything you have done to your car, and the date and odometer reading at which it was done. Your glove-compartment notebook will serve as the record of dates of service, and spaces are provided after each of the maintenance lists for the mileages at which the work listed there was done. Since you will occasionally have repairs or replacements made that are not included in the maintenance lists because their life-expectancy cannot be predicted, or have work done at times different from those anticipated in the maintenance lists, spaces are provided at convenient intervals for "Unscheduled Repairs." So when you have the front brakes overhauled, for example, or the stater replaced, enter the repair and the date and odometer reading in one of these spaces. You may think you will remember that you had this important job or that one done, and approximately when; but unless you are particularly gifted, you probably won't remember either, and their is a good chance that you will really want to refer to a reliable record at some time in the future.

## Five Things To Have Checked Monthly

It will take you fifteen minutes, at most.

During your first gasoline stop of each month, have the following things checked:

1. **Engine oil level.** Most engines "use oil." Even if your engine never needs oil between changes, the level should be checked at least once a month, in case the situation should change. If the engine needs oil as often as once a month, have the level checked more frequently.

2. **Coolant Level.** This level may drop as a result of evaporation or leaking, and engine overheating could result.

3. **Tire pressure.** If the tires are not sufficiently inflated, they may be dangerous at highway speeds; and in any case they will wear out prematurely.

4. **Battery electrolyte level,** if your battery has inspection caps (which "sealed" batteries do not have.) The electrolyte level drops as a result of evaporation. Battery damage may result if the level is not maintained.

5. **Power steering fluid** (if your car has a power-steering system). Leakage causes this level to drop. The power-steering pump may be damaged if the level drops too low.

## And one thing more for YOU to do:

Run the **air-conditioning unit** (if you have one) at the maximum "cold" setting and maximum fan speed for five minutes each month, to lubricate the seals.

## Special "High-Frequency" List

Enter below any maintenance services that should, according to your owner's manual, be performed more frequently than every 5,000 miles. Review your owner's manual particularly carefully if your car has a *diesel engine* or *front-wheel drive* or both.

*Diesel-engine note:* Present-day diesel engines require oil changes at the beginning of the summer season and at the beginning of the winter season that are not related to car mileage.

| *Service* | *Frequency* |
| --- | --- |
| _____ | _____ |
| _____ | _____ |
| _____ | _____ |

## 5,000-Mile List

Every 5,000 miles, have the following done:

1. Change engine oil
2. Chassis lube
3. Inspect brake lines (and transmission-cooler lines if it is an automatic-transmission car)
4. Inspect front tires for abnormal wear
5. Inspect axle dust boots (transaxle cars)
6. Check carburetor warm-up device
7. Check all fluid levels
8. Check electrical-system and battery condition
9. Check all belts and hoses
10. Check coolant antifreeze content
11. Check distributor dwell angle (breaker-point ignition)
12. Oil door hinges and clutch and transmission linkages

*For your own information:*

1.  Engine oil becomes contaminated with grit, gasoline, water, and sludge.

2.  "Chassis lube" refers to the lubricating of ball joints and other hinged joints in the suspension system and the steering system and the universal joints if they can be lubricated.

3.  Brake lines and hoses supply brake fluid to the brake assemblies at the wheels and transmission-cooler lines carry transmission fluid to the radiator and back to the transmission. Any leakage at all in either system will cause trouble, and should be detected as early as possible. When the car is up on the grease rack for oil-change it is a simple matter to investigate the lines for rock-damage, leakage, etc.

4.  The cause of abnormal tire wear should be corrected promptly to avoid premature wearing-out of tires. Front-end alignment and worn-out shock absorbers are possible causes.

5.  Water and dirt in the drive linkage can cause serious damage to the transaxle assembly.

6.  See pages 69 and 72 for descriptions of carburetor heaters.

7.  The list includes transmission oil, transmission fluid, brake fluid, clutch hydraulic fluid, power-steering fluid, differential oil and air-conditioner refrigerant.

8.  Check electrical-system voltage and battery electrolyte level.

9.  The water-pump belt and the alternator belt—often a single belt—and the power-steering belt (if your car is so equipped) should be replaced promptly if in doubtful condition. Other belts drive the air-conditioner compressor and the air-injection-reactor pump. Radiator and heater hoses are checked for physical damage, deterioration, and seeping joints.

10. The ethylene glycol content of the coolant mixture must be high enough to prevent freezing in winter and boiling-over in hot weather.

11. Distributor breaker points must be adjusted to compensate for wear; failure to do so will result in unsteady engine operation, or even make the engine inoperative.

12. Generally speaking, lubrication of hinges and linkages is important primarily as a matter of owner morale—which is a very important matter.

*Enter the odometer reading in the spaces provides below, each time you have the services on the 5,000-mile list performed:*

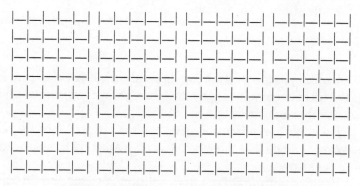

## Unscheduled and Off-Schedule Repairs

Write down repairs and replacements made at times other than called for by the maintenance lists, or are not included in the maintenance lists at all. Record dates and odometer readings for each entry.

_____

_____

_____

### 10,000-Mile List

Every 10,000 miles have the following done, *in addition to* the things on the 5,000-mile list:

1. Replace the engine oil filter
2. Replace the fuel filter (diesel cars)
3. Replace the spark plugs (but see note 3, below)
4. Check the air filter
5. Clean the battery posts
6. Rotate the tires
7. Inspect the brake linings (but see note 7, page 37)
8. Check under-side for safety: steering linkages, suspension joints, floor pan, frame.

*For your information:*

1. In doing its job of straining dirt and sludge out of the engine oil, the filter becomes clogged and then permits unfiltered oil to circulate through the engine.

2. Fuel-injection pumps of diesel engines are protected by very fine-grained filters that must be replaced frequently to assure adequate fuel flow.

3. Engines with *breaker-point* ignition systems should have new spark plugs at 10,000-mile intervals to avoid deterioriation in fuel economy. Spark plugs and spark-plug leads of *electronic-ignition* cars should be inspected every 10,000 miles and replaced when necessary.

4. A clogged air filter increases fuel consumption.

5. The battery posts accumulate a layer of lead sulfate that impedes the flow of current and makes the battery behave as though it is weak or even dead.

6. Both the geometry of the car suspension system and the geometry of roadway surfaces cause the individual tires to have different wear patterns. Equalizing wear yields maximum tire mileage.

7. Brake linings usually need no attention for their first 20,000 miles of city driving or 30,000 miles of country or turnpike driving, and so this item can be omitted for an appropriate interval after you have had brakes overhauled.

8. The floor pan of a *unitized body* (or "unibody") car is particularly susceptible to serious corrosion damage. Steering linkages and suspension joints require no attention during the car's first 25,000 miles.

*Each time you have the services on the 10,000-mile list performed, enter the odometer reading below:*

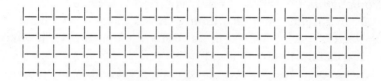

### Unscheduled and Off-Schedule Repairs

_____

_____

_____

_____

### 15,000-Mile List

Every 15,000 miles have the following done, *in addition to* the things on the 5,000-mile list:

1. Replace distributor points, condenser,and rotor (breaker-point ignition systems only)
2. Check timing

3. Inspect automatic choke
4. Replace fuel filter (fuel-injection gasoline cars)
5. Check PCV system
6. Clean or replace crankcase ventilation air filter
7. Check front-end alignment
8. Check clutch-pedal travel (manual-transmission cars)
9. Check emission-control devices

*For your own information:*

1. A malfunctioning breaker-point system causes the engine to run unsteadily and wastefully, or even to not run at all. *Electronic ignition* systems do not require this service.

2. In gasoline engines, "timing" refers to the sychronization of electric spark with piston position; in diesel engines it refers to the instant fuel is injected into the cylinder.

3. Gasoline fuel-injection pumps are protected by fine-grained filters that must be replaced frequently to assure adequate fuel flow.

4. If the Positive Crankcase Ventilation (PCV) valve or connecting hose becomes plugged, the engine will run unsteadily and wastefully, and may consume engine oil excessively.

5. Some cars have a separate filter for air that enters the crankcase through a "breather cap." If plugged, this filter can cause the same symptoms as a plugged PCV valve.

6. Road shocks and wear of suspension joints and steering linkages cause the front wheels to stray from proper alignment, resulting in excessive tire wear.

7. Some clutch systems, but not all, require periodic adjustment to compensate for wear of the clutch faces. If they are allowed to get too far out of adjustment, the wear rate increases markedly.

8. Some of the emission-control devices are mentioned specifically in the maintenance schedules. Others are the *early fuel evaporation (EFE) system*, the *hot-idle compensator*, the *fuel-cut solenoid*, the *exhaust gas recirculating (EGR) system*, the *air-injection reactor system*, and the *catalytic converter*.

*Each time you have the services on the 15,000-mile list performed, enter the odometer reading below:*

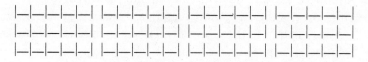

### Unscheduled and Off-Schedule Repairs

_____

_____

_____

_____

_____

### 25,000-Mile List

Every 25,000 miles have the following done, *in addition to* the things on the 5,000-mile list:

1. Replace all belts
2. Replace radiator and heater hoses
3. Replace air filter and carbon-canister filter
4. Replace fuel filter (carburetor-equipped engines)
5. Replace distributor cap

6. Replace antifreeze
7. Service automatic transmission
8. Check electronic ignition system
9. Pack non-driving-wheel bearings

*For your own information:*

1. A failed water-pump belt will shut you down, and a failed alternator belt may also. Other important belts (if your car is so equipped) are included in the air-injection-reactor, power-steering, air-conditioner, and diesel-car vacuum systems.

2. A leak in any of these hoses will result in engine overheating and engine shutdown.

3. A dirty air filter wastes fuel, and a plugged canister filter (page 65) prevents proper venting of the fuel system.

4. The fuel filter must be replaced periodically to assure adequate gasoline flow to the carburetor.

5. A deteriorated distributor cap permits leakage of ignition current, which wastes fuel or even prevents the engine from running.

6. Antifreeze becomes corrosive as a result of oxidation.

7. Details of servicing depend upon the design of the transmission.

8. An electronic ignition system does not ordinarily require servicing, but it should be checked periodically to assure that it is working properly.

9. "Pack" means lubricate.

*Each time you have the services on the 25,000-mile list performed, enter the odometer reading below:*

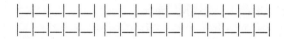

## 50,000-Mile List

Every 50,000 miles have the following done, *in addition to* the things on the 5,000-mile, 10,000-mile, and 25,000-mile lists:

1. Replace alternator and voltage regulator
2. Replace spark-plug leads (breaker-point ignition systems)
3. Replace radiator cap
4. Replace fuel pump
5. Clean battery cable connections to engine and starter

*For your own information:*

1. Deteriorated insulation permits high-voltage ignition current to by-pass the spark plugs, especially in damp weather, causing the engine to run unsteadily and be balky about starting.
2. A leaky radiator cap permits excessive loss of coolant by evaporation.
3. If you have had to replace the fuel pump within the past 50,000 miles, ignore this item.
4. Corrosion products at these connections increase electrical resistance, and even slightly increased resistance causes the starter to operate sluggishly, as though battery or starter is failing.

*Each time you have the services on the 50,000-mile list performed, enter the odometer readings below:*

### 75,000-Mile List

Every 75,000 miles have the following done, *in addition to* the things on the 5,000-mile, 15,000-mile, and 25,000-mile lists:

Replace the water pump and thermostat

*For your own information:*

Both of these items usually, but not always, last longer than 75,000 miles, but it is nevertheless prudent to replace them, as a precautionary measure, after not more than 75,000 miles.

*Enter below the odometer readings at which you have the above replacements made:*

|—|—|—|—|—| |—|—|—|—|—|

### Unscheduled and Off-Schedule Repairs

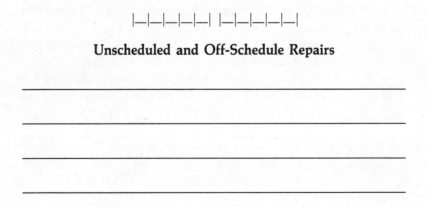

### 100,000-Mile List

Every 100,000 miles, have the following done, *in addition to* the things on the 5,000-mile, 10,000-mile, 25,000-mile, and 50,000-mile lists:

1. Replace the spark coil
2. Replace the ignition switch
3. Drain and refill manual transmission (but see note 3, below)
4. Drain and refill differential (but see note 4, below)

*For your own information:*

1. Although the coil may last longer, it is prudent to replace it after 100,000 miles.
2. Contact points inside the ignition switch deteriorate in their service in the starting system.
3. This item is included as a reminder if your owner's manual fails to specify a shorter interval for oil changes.
4. This item is included for the same reason as item 3, above.

*Enter below the odometer readings at which you have these things done:*

### NOTES

# Your Car

You don't need to know how a car works to have it well taken care of, but some people find that once they establish a relationship with a car—in some respects like a relationship with a person—they want to know more about it. This section is an introduction to the subject.

The descriptions and explanations here are simplified. We have not attempted to be complete or profound; rather, we have tried to include only enough in each description to indicate the general principle involved and to show a little about how it is applied in this case. We have probably missed this goal on both sides and included some descriptions that are too detailed and some that are too general and vague. For these mistakes in judgment, we apologize in advance. Our primary purpose has been to give enough information to interest the somewhat-interested readers, but not so much as to intimidate them.

You will not find here a description of everything in every make of automobile, or even everything in your own particular automobile. There are dozens of new devices that appear on this car or that, and even on standard models there are many complicated details that we do not try to cover. The important ones on your car will be mentioned—perhaps even described—in your owner's manual, and in any case your mechanic will be able to guide you in their maintenance.

It is unlikely that you will want—or be able—to read this section from beginning to end. It is primarily for reference and for browsing, to be used in connection with the Maintenance Schedules, list of Behavior Problems and the Index.

If your interest in your car should grow to the point where you are tempted to tackle some of the maintenance work yourself—millions of people succumb regularly to this temptation, and more power to them—you should arm yourself with a more detailed manual than this pretends to be. Your public library contains many such books, and from the array there or in a bookstore you can select one or several suited to your level of interest and ambition. If you find the subject at all compelling, then you should buy the shop manual for your make and model of car. Shop manuals can ordinarily be obtained for at least five years and sometimes for as long as ten years, after the model year. The parts department of any authorized dealer for your make of car will either order a shop manual for you or tell you how to order it for yourself.

## THE STARTING SYSTEM

The starting system cranks the engine to make it start. The system consists of the *battery* and *battery cables*, the *starter* with a *solenoid switch* to turn it on and off, and also a *switch* operated by the ignition key. If the car has an automatic transmission, the system includes a *neutral safety switch* that prevents the starter from operating except when the transmission lever is in the "neutral" or the "park" position. The next sketch shows the arrangement of these components. Some manual-transmission cars have a *clutch interlock* which permits the starter to operate only when the clutch pedal is fully depressed.

The **Starter,** or **Starting Motor,** is a very powerful electric motor that might be suitable for use on a crane or derrick, for lifting heavy loads. It rotates the flywheel and the other moving parts of the engine, and enables the engine to start.

The starter itself does not require routine maintenance. Its life expectancy cannot be expressed in miles because mileage is not what wears it out: starting the engine is what wears it out, and

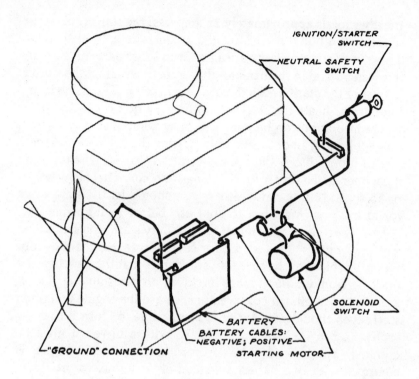

IGNITION/STARTER SWITCH

NEUTRAL SAFETY SWITCH

SOLENOID SWITCH

"GROUND" CONNECTION

BATTERY
BATTERY CABLES: NEGATIVE; POSITIVE
STARTING MOTOR

*Starting System*

the more often you start your engine, the sooner it will wear out. If you average, say, 5 or 6 starts a day, it would be 20 years before your starter accumulated the wear equal to a salesman's starter in two years. Don't count on 20 years' service from your starter, but 5 years is quite ordinary.

The starter differs from all other electrical devices on the automobile in the sheer magnitude of the electrical current it requires. A comparison with other major current-users shows this clearly: the generator working at its hardest generates 30-50 amperes; the current to the headlights and all the other lights together totals approximately 15 amperes; the starter, under ordinary conditions, needs 100-250 amperes to start the engine. These very large currents are a factor in other parts of the starting system, and in the troubles that sometimes afflict the starter.

One of the starter afflictions is *overheating*. The heavy starting current heats the starting motor very quickly to the point where insulation can be damaged or windings actually melted. ("I kept having all of this trouble starting the engine—and then, just to top it all off, the *starter* went!") If for some reason you must operate the starter for as long as 10 seconds in cold weather, or 15 seconds in warm weather, you should let the starter rest for at least two minutes, to cool off, before trying again.

*Diesel engines* require much heavier-duty starting systems than gasoline engines. This is true for several reasons, the most obvious of which, to the casual bystander, is that the diesel engine must be cranked *much* more briskly than a gasoline engine, if it is to start at all. (In cold weather, a gasoline engine will often start, even though the starter is barely able to "turn it over"—"ruh . . . ruh . . . ruh . . ." Not so with a diesel: it must be cranked "ruh-ruh-ruh-ruh." Accordingly, a diesel engine is equipped with two batteries instead of only one, to provide a double store of energy for starting, and a much heavier-duty starting motor than is used on gasoline engines of equal size. (The heavier-duty starting motors can be operated for stretches as long as 20-30 seconds without overheating seriously—and sometimes they have to be, in order to start the engine.)

## How to Talk About Your Starter Problems

• When you turn the ignition key to "start," and you hear nothing but a click, tell your mechanic "The solenoid just goes click; the starter isn't cranking the engine."

• When the starter goes "ruh-ruh-ruh" but the engine won't start, say "The starter is working but the engine doesn't start."

• When you hear a loud clashing noise, as of steel against steel, when you operate the starter, say "The starter gear clashes."

The **Starter Solenoid,** or **Solenoid Switch,** is a heavy-duty electric switch that turns the starting motor on and off. This is *not* the "start" switch you activate by turning the ignition key. The key-operated switch is a light-duty switch, as is (for example) the switch on a table lamp. The solenoid switch, on the other hand, is a very heavy-duty switch, as is (for example) the main switch that feeds current to an entire house.

The two switches work like this: when you turn the ignition key to "start," a current of about 40 amperes flows to the solenoid switch. This relatively small current causes the solenoid switch to slam shut, and a current of, say, 175 amperes then flows through the starting motor. The previous sketch shows a solenoid switch in the main line from the battery to the starter, and an ignition/starter switch connected to the solenoid.

The solenoid switch does not require any routine maintenance. Like the starting motor, its life expectancy depends upon the number of starts rather than the number of miles, or number of elapsed months or years. Considerable sparking occurs each time the solenoid switch is closed to permit the heavy current to flow, and each time it is opened to halt the current; it is thus subject to a good deal of pitting and corrosion, called "burning." The solenoid switch is likely to have to be replaced sooner than the starter—after perhaps three or four years in ordinary service instead of five. The solenoid switch will ordinarily give some warning by merely clicking when you turn the key to "start," rather than causing the starting motor to operate in its normal fashion. Be alert to such behavior. Ordinarily, after the solenoid has behaved that way the first time, the starter will operate the second or third time you try it. But this does not mean that the trouble has cured itself; it means that sometime soon the starter will *not* operate the second or third time you try it. Take it to your mechanic after the first or second warning.

When the **Ignition Switch** is turned to the "start" position, it serves as part of the starting system (it activates the starter

solenoid) and also as part of the ignition system, which is described in a later chapter.

The ignition-switch contact points suffer some sparking each
time the starter is operated, and it, like the solenoid switch, is
susceptible of failure after long service. The ignition switch should
be replaced as a precautionary measure every 100,000 miles.

The **Neutral Safety Switch,** or the **Clutch Interlock,** is intended
to safeguard against starting the engine when the car is in gear.
On cars with automatic transmission the safety switch permits
the starter to operate only if the transmission is set in either
"neutral" or "park." Not all cars with manual transmission have
clutch-interlock switches, but on those that do, the switch permits the starter to operate only if the clutch pedal is fully
depressed.

Both kinds of safety switches can get out of adjustment. If the
starter won't operate, it may sometimes be induced to do so by
moving the transmission lever slightly to the right or to the left
of the "neutral" or the "park" position, or (in the case of a manual-
transmission car) by letting up slightly on the clutch pedal. If
the starter responds to such measures, it tells you the safety switch
needs adjusting. This is a simple job, and you should have it done
fairly promptly for two reasons: first, the switch may slip further out of adjutsment and become entirely inoperative; and
second, sparking occurs when you search out the proper position of shift lever or clutch pedal, and the switch points are not
designed for such service.

Unless it has been operated for considerable periods when out
of adjustment, the neutral safety switch or the clutch interlock
switch is not likely to fail during the lifetime of the car, but since
the safety switch is in the same circuit with the key-operated
switch and the solenoid switch, it, too, is suspect when the other
switches are under suspicion.

The **Battery** is discussed later in connection with the charging system.

**Battery Cables,** which are also discussed later, are important to the operation of the starter. Because of the magnitude of the current required by the starter, the battery cables are big, heavy wires. If they did not have to supply the starter, they could be wires of much smaller size.

It is particularly important that all connections between the battery and the starter be clean and tight. The battery posts should be cleaned at regular intervals. In addition and just as important, the battery cable connections at the ends away from the battery should also be detached, thoroughly cleaned, and replaced, every 50,000 miles. One of these cables goes to the solenoid; the other cable goes to "ground" (see below). If your starter should become sluggish—if, for example, it seems to labor excessively when you re-start the engine when it is hot—one of the first things to suspect is a corroded ground connection. In fact, corrosion at the battery-cable connections can cause the starter to fail entirely; even a small amount of electrical resistance at any of these connections will reduce the voltage to the starter to the point where it will not be capable of cranking the engine.

---

### What "Ground" Means

Virtually all stationary electrical systems—in homes and factories, for example— are "grounded;" that is, they are connected at some point to the ground, usually for reasons of safety. Automobile electrical components are grounded by connecting them to the frame of the automobile, or to any metal object that is bolted directly to the frame: the engine, the body, or metal parts inside the body. In most automobile circuits, current flows from the battery through a wire to a component; the current then goes through the component, doing whatever work it is required to do; it then returns to the battery "through ground." Thus, "ground" completes most electrical circuits in an automobile.

A sluggish starter should be attended to at your next scheduled maintenance stop, or even sooner if the sluggishness is pronounced. A starting motor draws very large currents when it tries to crank an engine and inadequate voltage is supplied to it. Excessive currents generate excessive heat in the starter, and excessive heat causes damage and the damage is cumulative.

Some automobiles with large engines have a specific starter problem that baffles many mechanics: when the engine is hot, as for example after going through city traffic on a hot day, the starter is very sluggish or even entirely incapable of cranking the engine. In some cases, at least, the problem can be solved by installing a new negative battery cable—the "ground" cable—to connect the battery directly to the case of the starter. Theoretically, it should be adequate to ground the battery to the engine block, but in some engines this appears not to be adequate, after all. If you encounter persistent starter problems of this kind, it will certainly be worthwhile to try the direct-grounding treatment. If the experiment works, the result is gratifying; if it doesn't, it is not a very expensive failure.

## THE ENGINE

The engine provides the power for the automobile. The basic power-generating operation, combustion, takes place here.

The engine consists of the *cylinder block* (or *engine block*), the *cylinders*, the *cylinder head* (or *heads*), the *pistons*, the *connecting rods*, the *crankshaft*, the *crankcase*, the *flywheel* and the *camshaft*. In addition, the engine contains a *lubricating system* that delivers oil under pressure to lubricate all its moving parts.

Several other systems, which are described separately under their own functions, are essential to the operation of the engine or to protect it from damage: the fuel system, the ignition system (in gasoline engines only), the cooling system, and the exhaust system. Without these, the engine would be useless. Taken together with the engine itself, they comprise the power plant of the automobile.

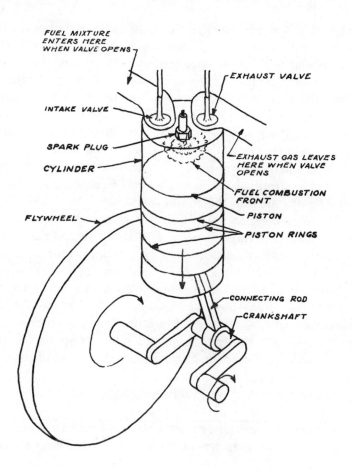

FUEL MIXTURE ENTERS HERE WHEN VALVE OPENS

EXHAUST VALVE

INTAKE VALVE

SPARK PLUG

CYLINDER

EXHAUST GAS LEAVES HERE WHEN VALVE OPENS

FUEL COMBUSTION FRONT

FLYWHEEL

PISTON

PISTON RINGS

CONNECTING ROD

CRANKSHAFT

*The Basic Operation*

*The basic operating cycle* of a gasoline engine goes like this: a mixture of gasoline vapor and air is sucked into a cylinder through the intake manifold and the intake valve; the valve closes; a piston inside the cylinder moves upward and compresses the gasoline-air mixture; the compressed fuel mixture is then ignited by a spark from a spark plug; the fuel mixture expands explosively when it is ignited; the explosion pushes the piston and its connecting rod downward; this moves the crankshaft, which turns the flywheel. Think of your foot and leg pushing down on the pedal of a bicycle; it is the same kind of motion. At the same time, the exhaust valve opens and allows the burned gases to escape through the exhaust manifold; the piston moves upward again; the exhaust valve closes. This completes the cycle. The intake valve opens as the piston starts down again, and the cycle is repeated. The preceding sketch illustrates this basic operation. (The **stratified charge engine** uses a second intake valve to admit extra air into the combustion chamber.)

The **diesel engine** operates in the same way as the gasoline engine except in three respects. First: only air is sucked into the cylinder, rather than a mixture of gasoline vapor and air. Second: the fuel (not gasoline, but a liquid similar to charcoal-lighter fluid) is squirted into the cylinder, rather than sucked in along with the air. Third: there is no spark plug; the fuel is ignited spontaneously when it is squirted into the very hot compressed air in the cylinder, rather than being ignited by an electric spark. The result of combustion is the same in the two kinds of engine. The explosive burning pushes the piston and its connecting rod downward, turning the crankshaft, and so on.

An automobile engine has several cylinders and pistons, usually four or six or eight, depending on the design; each piston applies downward force on the crankshaft. The next sketch shows the location of cylinders (shaded lines), pistons, crankshaft, and flywheel inside an engine. Since the pistons fire in sequence, one after the other, very rapidly, the crankshaft is always being turned by one or another of the pistons.

The **Engine Block** is the main body of the engine. All the working parts of the support systems are attached to the block.

A **Cylinder** in an automobile engine is a cylindrical hole bored through the engine block. In four- and six-cylinder engines, the holes are almost always bored in a longitudinal row; in an eight-cylinder engine, the cylinders are in two rows of four each, oriented in the form of a V, so as to point to a common crankshaft: hence the term "V-8."

The **Cylinder Head** is a slab of metal that is bolted onto the top of the engine block to provide caps for the cylinders. A V-8 engine has two cylinder heads, one for each bank of four cylinders. The cylinder head always contains threaded holes into which the spark plugs are screwed if it is a gasoline engine, or glow-plugs if it is a diesel engine. And it usually contains the intake and exhaust valves as well. Built into the cylinder head of a diesel engine is a small "pre-combustion chamber"—a small dome-shaped cavity—into which the fuel is squirted, and where the combustion of fuel and hot compressed air begins. The cylinder head is labeled in the sketch.

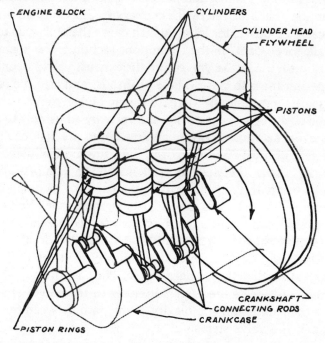

*Location of cylinders, pistons, crankshaft and flywheel in an engine.*

**Engine Valves** are flat disks with beveled circumferences and vertical central stems, like mushrooms. Valves are included among the basic parts of an engine shown on page 53, and they are shown in greater detail, in connection with a discussion of valves in the Definitions. Engine valves fit into beveled circular holes ("valve ports") in the cylinder head when they are closed, and are pushed clear of the holes when they are open, allowing the gasoline-air fuel mixture, or the exhaust gas mixture, as the case may be, to flow through. Heavy valve springs cause the valves to close; they are caused to open in the proper sequence by the valve gear an assemly of cams, pushrods, and rocker arms. Part of the valve gear is attached to the upper side of the cylinder head; a **valve cover** made of sheet steel, covers the valve gear to keep lubricant in, and dirt and water out.

The **Camshaft** in most automobile engines is a longitudinal bar deep inside, that is driven by the crankshaft. The camshaft is fitted with cans, or off-center lobes, which cause the pushrods to rise and fall. (See "Cam" in the Definitions section.) The pushrods, in turn, push the intake valves and the exhaust valves open, and then permit them to close. These pushrods, and also the rocker arms, suffer as a result of this activity, and when they wear they become noisy; it is essential that the valve be adjustable to compensate for this wear. **Hydraulic Valve Lifters** are included in the valve gear of most American cars; they automatically and continuously make the needed adjustments to compensate for pushrod wear. If hydraulic valve lifters are not included in the system, then the pushrods have adjustable ends, called **Valve Tappets;** these require periodic adjustment to reduce valve noise. Some systems have both adjustable tappets and hydraulic lifters.

In **Overhead Cam** engines, the camshaft is at the top of the engine, rather than buried deep inside. The basic purpose of this position is to locate the camshaft closer to the valves and thus reduce the length and complexity of the path between the camshaft and the valve stems.

**Pistons** are plugs that travel up and down inside the cylinders; they resemble inverted cylindrical drinking glasses, three to four inches in diameter (depending on the size of the engine) and of about equal height.

**Piston Rings** are spring-steel narrow rings that are mounted in grooves around the pistons. They press against the cylinder walls to seal against leakage around the pistons, to prevent loss of pressure following combustion. There are usually three rings on each piston.

**Connecting Rods** are links between the pistons and the crankshaft. A wrist pin attaches the connecting rod to the piston; this is a horizontal rod that goes through the piston from side to side, and through a hole in the upper end of the connecting rod.

The **Crankshaft** is a heavy steel shaft at the base of the engine that is turned by the downward thrust of the pistons and connecting rods acting rapidly and in sequence. This turning motion is transmitted to the **Drive Train** (see page 107) which ultimately turns the wheels and moves the automobile. Each crank on the crankshaft accommodates one connecting rod, except in a V-8 engine, where each crank is connected to a pair of cylinders.

The **Flywheel** is a heavy steel disk mounted at the rear of the crankshaft. It provides momentum and thus assures smooth rotation of the crankshaft. It also serves as the connecting link between the engine and the drive train.

The **Intake Manifold** is a heavy steel assembly with ducts branching from it, that is bolted onto the top or the side of the engine block to provide passageways from a central distribution point at the top of the manifold to the intake valves of each cylinder. Air or air-fuel mixture flows through these passageways, as explained in greater detail in the section on the **Fuel System**.

The **Exhaust Manifold** is a similar heavy steel duct assembly that is bolted onto the side of the engine or cylinder head, to provide passageways for exhaust gases to be conducted away from the exhaust valves. The passageways come together in a common duct onto which the exhaust pipe is bolted. The section about the **Exhaust System** begins on page 77, and the location of the exhaust manifold is shown in the sketch following that page.

The **Engine Lubrication System** consists of an oil reservoir, called the crankcase, an oil pump, an oil filter, and an elaborate system of ducts and passages to all of the moving engine parts. The function of the engine lubricating system is to keep all of the moving parts of the engine bathed in oil or oil mist at all times when the engine is running. It must not fail in this function; if oil were not delivered to the moving parts in adequate quantity, it would be only a few minutes before the engine either labored to a halt or produced heavy thudding sounds that would betoken serious trouble to even an inexperienced ear.

The **Crankcase** is the lower half of the engine; it encloses the crankshaft, camshaft, and oil pump, and serves as the oil reservoir for the engine. The bottom of the crankcase is called the **oil pan.**

The **Dipstick** is the steel rod or strip with a ring or hook at the top that projects downward through a hole at the base of the engine into the crankcase. It is used for measuring the depth of the oil in the crankcase. Some cars have an **Oil Level Gauge** on the instrument panel. The gauge indicates the level of a float that rides on the surface of the oil in a small auxiliary oil reservoir interconnected with the pool of oil in the crankcase.

The **Oil Pump** is a simple pump located in the crankcase. Driven by the crankshaft or the camshaft, it sucks up oil from the crankcase, and pumps it through the lubricating system. When the engine is operating at ordinary driving speed, the oil pressure in the system in most engines is in the range 20-40 pounds per square inch—in the normal range of household water pressure. When the engine is idling and hot, the pressure may drop as low as 5-10 pounds per square inch.

The **Oil Filter** is a strainer, located outside the crankcase where it is easily accessible. The oil travels from the oil pump through the filter before going on to the moving parts. The function of the filter is to strain out of the oil all the dirt, sludge, gums, etc., that would aggravate wear of the moving parts. The oil filter is provided with a filter by-pass that permits the oil to bypass the filter if it should become clogged with the impurities it captures. The reason for this is that although feeding unfiltered oil to the moving parts may cause unnecessary wear, cutting off the flow of oil entirely, because of a clogged filter, would be disastrous.

**Oil Passages** lead to all the moving parts of the engine and through many of them to supply oil to surfaces that cannot otherwise be reached. Thus, for example, the crankshaft is drilled with holes that receive oil from bearings in which the shaft rotates. This permits the oil to go to the connecting rods; the connecting rods are drilled with holes that conduct the oil on to the wrist pins; and the holes in the wrist pins conduct oil on to the cylinder walls. The oil is under pressure, and so it squirts from all the joints and bearings and is whipped into a mist by the moving parts. It ultimately falls back into the reservoir of oil in the crankcase, where it is picked up by the oil pump and returned to the engine—and so on, around and around.

The **Oil Pressure Indicator Light** or **Oil Pressure Gauge** is the most important item on your instrument panel because it notifies you if the oil pressure drops to a dangerous level. If you have an oil gauge, develop the habit of glancing at it regularly whenever the engine is running, including when it is idling. At moderate or high speeds, the gauge hand normally points somewhere in the range of 10 o'clock to 1 o'clock, depending on the temperature of the engine (the hotter the engine, the lower the oil pressure); at idling speeds, even when the engine is hot, the hand must be well away from the lower end of the scale. Experience will teach you what is "normal" at idling speeds.

If you have an **Indicator Light,** it will go on when your oil pressure drops to a dangerous level. It is essential that you develop the habit of glancing at the light when you turn on the ignition, before you turn the key to "start," to check on whether the light is working. It is *intended* to go on at that time briefly, to provide you with information about the condition of the light itself. If it does *not* go on at this time, it means that the bulb has burned out or that the warning system has failed in some way. It is important to have the bulb replaced, or the system repaired, immediately; an alarm system that is inoperative is worse than useless—it is dangerous.

Both kinds of oil-pressure indicators depend upon an **Oil-pressure Sending Switch** and wiring connections to the gauge or indicator light. The sending switch is screwed into one of the main oil passages in the engine.

### THE ENGINE MUST BE SHUT DOWN IMMEDIATELY IF THE OIL PRESSURE GAUGE READING DROPS ABNORMALLY, OR IF THE OIL WARNING LIGHT GOES ON.

You will run the risk of damaging the engine, perhaps beyond repair at reasonable cost, if you run it in defiance of an oil-pressure warning for more than a few seconds. If the oil level is substantially below the ADD OIL mark on the dipstick, you may only need a quart of oil to cure the problem—*but add the oil first,* and confirm that it restores things to normal, before proceeding. A mechanic may subsequently find, by connecting a pressure gauge to the system, that the pressure indicator has given you a wrong signal, and that the oil pressure is actually at a safe level; but until this is firmly established, you should assume that the oil pressure is *not* at a safe level. Once reassured on this point you may proceed normally, but you should have the warning system repaired as soon as possible, so that you will be warned if for some reason the oil pressure really does drop to a dangerous level—as it might, if the oil pump fails, or some part of the lubrication systems develops a major leak.

**Engine Maintenance.** The most important single item in engine maintenance is *lubrication*. Other systems—cooling, ignition, fuel exhaust—must also be kept in good operating condition in order to assure good performance of the engine, and these systems and their maintenance are discussed individually in later pages. But for the engine itself, oil is the crucial element.

As recently as about 1970 one could generalize about suitable engine oils for different climates, but in recent years innovations in engine design and oil formulation have imposed new lubrication requirements and provided new opportunities. For engine-oil recommendations, you should consult your owner's manual or a mechanic you trust. Owner's-manual recommendations are particularly important in the case of diesel engines, which require particularly heavy-duty oils and also require different grades of oil in winter and summer, respectively.

Except for the seasonal needs of diesel engines, engine oil and oil filter should be replaced on regular schedules. Whether they should both be replaced on the same schedule, and how frequently the replacements should be carried out, are subjects of disagreement among experts. Owner's-manual recommendations for gasoline engines range from "every 3,000 miles or every three months, whichever comes first," with the filter changed every other time, to "every 10,000 miles or every eight months," with the filter changed each time. Also, most manuals tell you to change oil more frequently if you use your car in "severe service"—without defining severe-service conditions clearly enough to make the recommendation useful.

Owner's-manual recommendations reflect the engineers' estimates of lubrication needs in "average" service, merged with the marketers' estimates of what the public will accept with some enthusiasm. A middle ground is defensible: change oil every 5,000 miles (but more frequently in the case of a diesel engine if the owner's manual says so), and change the oil filter every 10,000 miles (but every 5,000 miles in cars of vintage 1970 or older, in which the filtering of air to the crankcase is less effective than it is in later models).

**Engine Overhaul** means replacing or reconditioning all parts inside the engine that have become seriously worn after long service. These include the piston rings, pistons, crankshaft bearings, connecting rods, and (usually separately) engine valves and valve-gear components. This is a large undertaking, and after finding out how much this is going to cost, you may be tempted to decide that it's not worth spending that much money on an old car. DON'T GIVE IN TO THIS TEMPTATION without first studying the situation carefully.

In the first place, the symptoms that make you think the engine needs overhauling are also the symptoms of other problems, smaller and less expensive to solve. The two major symptoms of a worn-out engine are high oil consumption and blue smoke coming out of the tail pipe; but if the odometer reading is less than 100,000 miles when you become aware of the blue smoke and notice the high oil consumption, you almost certainly do *not* need an engine overhaul.

In the second place, even if your engine does need an overhaul, and you are stunned at what it is going to cost, look carefully at your alternative. Generally speaking, an engine can be completely overhauled for roughly one-tenth the cost of a new car of similar make and size. If you think you might buy, not a new car, but a newer car to replace your older one and to avoid the cost of an engine overhaul, think carefully; you would probably pay more in finance charges alone than the cost of the engine overhaul.

High **Oil Consumption** is indeed one of the symptoms of a worn-out engine. It can point to piston rings that are not doing their job—that is, not wiping oil from the cylinder walls when the pistons go down, allowing an excessive amount of oil to be burned, along with the fuel mixture, in the cylinders. But this is not the only route by which oil can escape from the system. It may simply leak out around oil seals where the crankshaft goes through the front wall or the rear wall of the crankcase, or under, or through, a gasket that is supposed to (but sometimes doesn't) make an oil-tight seal between the engine and some component that is bolted onto the engine; or through a cracked oil-pressure sending switch. A plugged-up PCV (positive crankcase ventilation) system can cause the air pressure inside the crankcase to be excessive and this pressure may force oil past the crankshaft oil seals, or past the piston rings, or under, or through, gaskets that would not leak at normal pressures. If your oil usage goes up, all of these items should be checked before you think of an engine overhaul.

**Blue Smoke,** likewise, can be a symptom of a worn-out engine; it means that oil is being burned in the cylinders. But the oil can get there by routes other than leaky piston rings. Oil can reach the cylinders also through the **valve stems** and leaking **valve seals.** The upper end of each valve stem, where it meets the rocker arm, is bathed in oil. Valve seals prevent this oil from being sucked into the cylinders, and there being burned, and thus generating blue smoke and also contributing to high oil consumption. So when your engine starts spewing blue smoke out the back, ask your mechanic to check the valve seals. They may need replacing and they are much less expensive than piston rings. **Black smoke** is caused by maladjustments or malfunction in the fuel system; it does not indicate oil consumption, but only an excessive concentration of fuel in the combustion mixture. Diesel systems are more likely to product black smoke than gasoline systems.

**Engine Valves** usually require overhauling sooner than piston rings, bearings, and other major components of the engine. The life-expectancy of valves is of the order of 100,000—125,000 miles. Your mechanic will probably be the first to detect valve trouble, because he will not be able to make the engine idle steadily when he tunes it up. And compression tests in previous tune-ups will have foreshadowed the trouble by revealing that one or more cylinders has lower compression than the others. Valves can be reconditioned rather than replaced; after reconditioning, they will last approximately half as long as new valves. If you buy new valves, the cost of the valve overhaul job will be increased by one-fourth to one-third; but it will be money well spent, since it will make it unnecessary to work on the valve system again for another 100,000 miles.

## THE FUEL SYSTEM

The fuel system delivers to the engine a precisely measured supply of fuel to provide the power the engine needs to do its job. The basic fuel system consists of a *fuel tank, fuel lines,* a *fuel pump,* a *fuel filter,* a *carburetor or other fuel-metering device,* an *intake manifold,* and an *air filter.* These basic elements are shown below. Numerous anti-pollution and operational control devices that have been developed in recent years are not shown in the sketch; they are described in the later pages of this chapter.

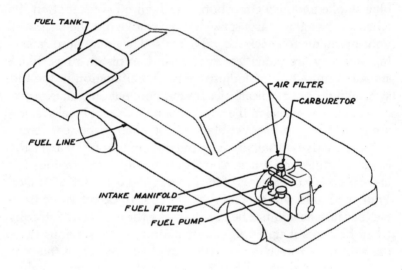

*A Fuel System*

The **Fuel Tank** is located at the rear of the car. Inside the tank is the fuel gauge tank unit that conveys information about the fuel level to the gauge on the instrument panel. This is done by means of a float that rides on the surface of the fuel; it is attached to a lever that swings up and down as the float rises or drops; and the lever operates a control knob that sends a faint electric current to the gauge. Most cars also have a fuel filter located inside the tank, and some have a fuel pump in the tank as well.

Fuel is delivered from the tank to the engine compartment through a **Fuel Line** that is secured to the frame of the car. As fuel is removed from the tank, air must be permitted to enter the tank to occupy the empty space. Cars made since the early Seventies have been equipped with a **Fuel Tank Vent Line,** a tube that leads from the air space of the fuel tank forward to the engine compartment (paralleling the fuel line) where it is connected to a **Carbon Canister,** which permits air to flow to the tank as needed. (The carbon canister is also described in a later paragraph.) Cars that do not have a carbon canister must use a **Vented Fuel Tank Cap**—i.e., a cap with a built-in air passage that permits the tank to "breathe"; use of a non-breathing cap is likely to result in a flattened fuel tank when the fuel pump removes fuel from the tank and creates a vacuum.

The **Fuel Pump** transfers fuel from the tank to a carburetor or fuel-injection pump in the engine compartment. The pump is usually bolted onto the engine and driven by a mechanical linkage to the engine, but some fuel pumps are powered by an independent electric motor. In either case, if the pump is located in the engine compartment it *sucks* fuel from the tank via the fuel line. In very hot weather, **Vapor Lock** can occur in gasoline cars, since gasoline boils at appreciably lower temperatures under partial vacuum. If fuel turns to vapor in the fuel line, the pump cannot deliver liquid fuel to the engine, and so the engine stops. To combat vapor lock, the fuel pump is sometimes located inside the fuel tank, where it is immersed in fuel, and thus delivers the fuel under pressure rather than under partial vacuum.

Fuel pumps usually give no prior warning before they fail—and shut the engine down. They usually, but not always, last as long as 50,000 miles; but unless your mechanic knows from personal experience that your kind of fuel pump lasts longer, it should be replaced at this point.

**Fuel Filters** screen out dirt in the fuel, to prevent its interfering with the free flow of fuel through the carburetor or fuel-injection pump and nozzles (described below), or even through the fuel line itself.

Dirt gets into fuel by many routes, and the extent of such contamination is largely a matter of luck. Whenever the cap is taken off the fuel tank at the filling station, dirt is invited in. Swirling breezes carry dust and grit, some of it from your own car and some from the surrounding roads and driveways. The nozzle of the station fuel pump collects dirt particles and drops them into your tank. Leaves, insects, and flying seeds can enter the fuel tank when the cap is off. The filling station's storage tanks receive dirt along with the fuel from its supply truck, which in turn picks it up from the distribution-center tanks and atmosphere.

A **Tank Filter,** sometimes called the **Sock Filter,** is located inside the fuel tank. It screens out any coarse particles—leaves, twigs, insects—that could plug the fuel line. In diesel systems, this filter also helps protect the fuel line from *precipitated wax* that forms in diesel fuel in particularly cold weather. (Some diesel-system fuel lines are equipped with electrical heaters to combat wax. If your diesel car doesn't have one, it can be added at modest cost.)

What mechanics commonly call "the fuel filter" is located at the engine end of the fuel line, just before the carburetor or the fuel-injection-pump assembly. Carburetors have numerous jets, orifices, and liquid passages of small diameter that must not be allowed to plug up; the fuel filter is fine-grained enough to trap dirt particles before they reach the carburetor—and in the process the filter becomes plugged. It should be replaced at 25,000-mile intervals. The fuel-metering system of a fuel-injection gasoline engine would be rendered inoperative by dirt particles that a carburetor could tolerate, and so the fuel filter for such engines is finer-grained than that for a conventional carburetor-equipped engine. It should be replaced at 15,000-mile intervals. And finally, diesel fuel-injection systems are most vulnerable of all: they require finer-grained filters than even the gasoline fuel-injection system, and these filters should be replaced every 10,000 miles.

Fuel tanks and fuel lines are subject to corrosion from water and road chemicals. Such internal corrosion can be mitigated or prevented by adequate underside rustproofing, as described on page 20. Water in the fuel causes external corrosion, and it is largely unpreventable. Moisture in the air condenses to liquid water in tanks throughout the fuel-distribution system, including your own fuel tank. (It is most unlikely that any filling station ever deliberately sells "watered" gasoline or diesel fuel. It would be technically difficult, and legally risky.) Corrosion leaks in fuel lines are not uncommon. Fortunately, fuel lines can be replaced at moderate cost. Fuel tanks, being made of heavier steel, seldom rust through; and some tanks are made of plastic, and—whatever their other shortcomings—they are immune to corrosion.

If water reaches the engine along with or instead of fuel, the engine will run unsteadily, if at all. Additives are available under several brand names that "dry" the gasoline by acting as a mutual solvent for gasoline and water.

The **Air Filter** is contained in the horizontal disk, 10-15 inches in diameter and 2-3 inches high, that is the biggest single thing you see when you open the hood. Its function is to screen out dirt in the air and thus protect the engine from abrasion. The air filter increases very significantly the intervals between engine overhauls.

The air filter should be inspected for fouling every 10,000 miles, and replaced if it is dirty; and in any case it should be replaced after 25,000 miles. In carburetor-equipped cars, a dirty air filter increases fuel consumption by causing excessive suction to be applied to the liquid fuel in the carburetor and thus causing fuel to flow into the air stream at an excessive rate. In fuel-injection cars, gasoline or diesel, a dirty filter distorts the air:fuel ratio, and reduces miles per gallon, by reducing the amount of air into which fuel is carefully metered by the fuel-injection system.

The **Early Fuel Evaporation (EFE) System** is an emissions-control device that maintains the temperature of the air going to the air filter at about 100° Fahrenheit for the purpose of enabling a gasoline engine to use a leaner, cleaner-burning air-fuel mixture than it could use if the air were colder. A **thermostatic vacuum switch** controls the position of a damper that permits heated air (which has passed over the exhaust manifold, the hottest part of the engine) with cold air from the engine compartment. The EFE system, like other emission-control devices, should be checked at 15,000-mile intervals for condition of valves and hoses.

A **Carburetor** is a device for mixing gasoline and air in the proportions needed by an internal-combustion engine at a given time for a given purpose. (An alternate system, fuel injection, is discussed on page 72.) An engine's fuel requirement varies widely with temperature, acceleration, and load: a cold engine requires a fuel mixture that is much richer in gasoline than does a hot engine, and when the intake air is cold, the mixture must be richer than when the air is warm; when you accelerate, the engine needs a higher concentration of gasoline, and in a hurry, than when you are cruising at a steady speed; and when the car is heavily loaded, the mixture must be richer than when the load is light. The carburetor must respond to all of these needs.

Basically, the principle of mixing air and gasoline in the automobile engine is a simple one, and it is seen at its simplest in a gasoline lawn-mower engine. Here, the engine sucks a stream of air through a duct; liquid gasoline dribbles through a small tube into the center of the air stream at a rate appropriate to the needs of the engine. The gasoline evaporates, and the mixture of air and gasoline vapor thus formed is the fuel mixture for the lawn-mower engine.

The mixing problem in an automobile is more complex because both the amount of fuel mixture and its composition (i.e., the concentration of gasoline vapor in the air) must be varied over wide ranges to accommodate the varying needs of the engine. The essential basic operation is the same as that described above, and the next sketch illustrates it. The pistons and valves, acting together, suck air through the carburetor body. (The intake manifold connects the carburetor with the cylinders and their pistons and valves). Gasoline in a reservoir (the "float chamber" in the sketch) flows through the carburetor jet and out into the stream, where ite vaporates to form the air-gasoline vapor mixture. The supply of gasoline in the float chamber is maintained at a very precise level by the **float valve:** if the level is too high, the float valve plugs the gasoline inlet line and the fuel pump cannot force additional gasoline into the float chamber; when the level drops the pump supplies additional gasoline.

A **Choke Valve** is located in the carburetor body just upstream of the tube that conveys liquid gasoline into the air stream. The function of the choke valve is to cause more gasoline than normal to be sucked into the air stream. It is a "butterfly" valve, similar to a damper in a chimney. The choke valve achieves the richer gasoline-air mixture the engine needs when it is cold by restricting the air flow through the carburetor body and thereby increasing the suction on the gasoline feed tube. Most carburetors are equipped with an **Automatic Choke:** the position of the damper is controlled by a temperature-sensitive coil spring that gradually opens the damper as the temperature of the air going to the carburetor increases. (On some engines, the temperature-sensitive element is activated by the temperature of the engine coolant.) In addition, most modern carburetors have some version of **vacuum break** mechanism that reponds to engine faltering by closing the choke somewhat, to reduce the tendency of the engine to stall during warm-up.

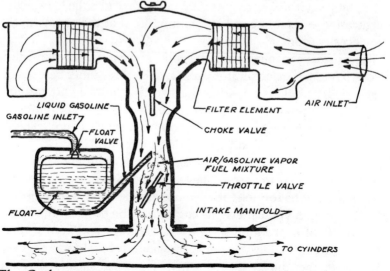

*The Carburetor*

The **Throttle Valve** is a second and more important damper in the air duct of the carburetor. This valve controls the rate of flow of the fuel mixture to the engine. Since the speed of the engine depends upon the amount of fuel that is admitted to the cylinders, the throttle valve controls the speed of the gasoline engine.

The **Accelerator Pedal** controls the throttle valve. When the accelerator pedal is up, the damper is turned cross-wise in the carburetor air duct and the flow of fuel mixture is very small; when the accelerator is "floored," the damper is "wide open" and the flow of fuel mixture is at maximum.

The complexities of the automobile carburetor as compared with the lawn-mower-engine carburetor are in the form of additional features that the lawn-mower engine does not require. The most prominent and most basic of these are the *acceleration pump* and the *choke unloader.*

The **Acceleration Pump** is a device in the carburetor that is similar to a water pistol. When a trigger is pulled, it squirts an extra charge of gasoline into the air stream going through the carburetor. If you push down on the accelerator pedal very slowly the trigger is not actuated; but if you push the pedal down rapidly the pump squirts. The acceleration pump provides the higher concentration of gasoline in the fuel mixture that the engine needs for acceleration.

The owner's manual that came with your car probably instructs you to pump the accelerator pedal two or three times before you try to start a cold engine. In other words, squirt liquid gasoline into the carburetor air duct, to load the air that goes into the cylinders with a high concentration of gasoline vapor. This is good procedure—provided you don't overdo it.

If you *do* overdo it, the **Choke Unloader** will come to your rescue. The choke unloader is never identified in owner's manuals, but instructions for activating it are almost always included. If for any reason you believe the engine may be *flooded*, then push the accelerator pedal all the way to the floor and *hold* it there (don't *pump* it!) while you crank the engine for up to five seconds, to see whether the engine will start. "Flooding" means excessive gasoline, in liquid or vapor form, in the cylinders. Excessive pumping on the accelerator pedal or a malfunctioning automatic choke can cause flooding. When you push the accelerator pedal down you squirt even more gasoline into the carburetor throat and the intake manifold, but no matter: when the pedal goes all the way to the floor it opens both the choke valve and the throttle valve wide; and as you crank with the accelerator pedal "floored," air flows through the carburetor and manifold and sweeps out excess gasoline.

*Percolation* can also cause flooding. If you shut down a hot engine for 15 minutes or so, it may be difficult to re-start for the next half-hour. The reason is that gasoline vapor from the hot carburetor fills the intake manifold. The choke unloader overcomes this king of flooding, too.

The automatic choke, the acceleration pump, and the choke unloader are all adjustable. The choke may need adjusting if you have to pump the accelerator pedal more than twice in order to start the cold engine, or if the engine persists in stalling after it has had 30 seconds or more to warm up. The more recent the vintage of your car, however, the greater is the array of emission-control devices that might, by malfunctioning, be the source of your starting-up difficulties.

On most carburetors, the ratio of air to fuel that is fed to the engine at idling speeds, the *"idling mixture,"* can be adjusted for optimum smoothness; but some carburetors manufactured after about 1976 are not adjustable: the idling mixture is set at the factory. Most carburetors can be adjusted for optimum idling *speed.* ("On-board" computers of computer-controlled cars adjust idling speed continuously, in accordance with programmed specifications. It causes a small electric motor to adjust the setting of a valve in the idle-mixture passage.) Too-slow idling causes the engine to stall excessively. Too-fast idling causes, at minimum, excessive wear of the clutch and other drive-train components; and if you have an automatic transmission the car lurches forward when you shift into "Drive," and creeps forward excessively at traffic lights, for example. A more troublesome effect of too-high idling speed is **after-run,** or **dieseling:** the engine refuses to stop running when you turn off the ignition. This problem is discussed further in the Ignition System chapter.

Some carburetors of recent vintage are equipped with anti-dieseling devices that cut off the flow of fuel-air mixture to the engine when you shut off the ignition switch. One such device is a **Fuel-Cut Solenoid,** which causes idle-mixture passages within the carburetor body to be closed, and another device is the **Idle Speed Solenoid,** which causes the throttle plate to close completely when the ignition is turned off. In each case, a spring causes a valve to snap shut unless it is held open by the solenoid, which is an electromagnetic device that responds to an electric current. Some carburetors are equipped with a **Hot-Idle Compensator,** which is a temperature-sensitive butterfly valve (similar in design to the automatic-choke valve) that admits extra air into the carburetor throat just upstream of the throttle plate when the engine is hot; its purpose is to "lean out" the fuel mixture as much as possible, to improve gasoline mileage and reduce unburned fuel in the exhaust.

**Fuel-Injection** systems used on gasoline engines use precisely-controllable metering valves and control systems of very advanced design instead of the array of floats, check valves, needle valves, and squirt-pumps of conventional carburetors. The arrangement can be pictured by referring to the sketch on page 69; assume that the choke valve, float chamber, and float are not there at all, but that instead the gasoline-inlet line is fitted with an electrically-operated valve, beyond which it continues on, horizontally, to a spray nozzle in the wall of the carburetor body. The gasoline in the supply line is under the pressure provided by the fuel pump; so if the injection valve can be controlled to permit a flow of gasoline appropriate to the prevailing needs of the engine (which vary widely as operating conditions change), this sytem can perform all of the functions of the several systems embodied in a carburetor.

Control of the injection valve can be achieved with present-day small, reliable, and relatively inexpensive **Microprocessors** (sometimes called *microcomputers* or *"on-board computers."*) Some fuel-injection cars have mechanical control systems which pre-dated the microprocessors, but the modern electronic control apparatus has made much more refined systems possible. The microprocessor is able to take into account a very wide array of conditions in arriving at optimum fuel-flow rate: air temperature, engine temperature, throttle setting, atmospheric pressure, oxygen content of the exhaust gas, and so on.

The **Carbon Canister** is a device that traps gasoline vapor that would otherwise pollute the atmosphere. The canister is located in the engine compartment. It is filled with a special charcoal that is capable of absorbing vapors of gasoline and similar substances. A **Carburetor Vent Tube**, a **Tank Vent Line**, and a **Canister Purge Tube** are all connected at one end of the canister, and the other end of the canister is open to the air. The vent tube leads from the air space above the liquid gasoline in the carburetor float chamber, the tank vent line leads from the air space above the liquid in the gasoline tank, and the purge tube is connected to a flow-restrictor fitting on the intake manifold. When the engine runs, a small flow of air sweeps through the canister, removing by evaporation any gasoline that has been absorbed by the charcoal when the engine was not running; meanwhile, fumes from both the carburetor and the fuel tank are recycled into the intake manifold.

Ventilation air must flow freely through the engine crankcase to carry away combustion products (called "blow-by") that the piston rings allow to pass into the crankcase. The supply of air for crankcase ventilation is usually drawn from the main air stream to the engine, just downstream of the air filter element. Contaminated air is not permitted to discharge into the atmosphere, but instead is recycled to the intake manifold through a one-way **Positive Crankcase Ventilation (PCV) Valve.** The PCV Valve, which is not very expensive, should be replaced at

15,000-mile intervals, and connecting hoses should be replaced if necessary. If the PCV valve fails to regulate the flow of ventilation air through the crankcase properly, the engine is likely to run unsteadily, particularly at low speeds. A malfunctioning PCV valve may also cause what appears to be an increase in oil-consumption by the engine, but is actually an increase in oil leakage. If the PCV valve permits excessive pressure to build up in the crankcase, oil seeps through gasketed joints and past seals around the crankshaft, camshaft, and valve seals.

The **Exhaust Gas Recirculation (E.G.R.) System** is an emission-control device that reduces the formation of nitrogen oxides in the combustion process in the cylinders. The EGR system recycles exhaust gas, which contains little if any oxygen, and mixes it in small proportions with the intake air in the intake manifold. The effect of this dilution is to reduce the oxygen content of the combustion mixture, and thus reduce the combustion temperature in the cylinders and correspondingly the formation of nitrogen oxides. The EGR system should be checked for operating condition every 15,000 miles. Malfunctioning of this system can cause stalling and rough operation of the engine under both idling and load conditions.

All diesel engines use fuel-injection fuel systems. A diesel engine has no spark plugs: combustion of the fuel-air mixture in the cylinders is caused not by an electric spark, but simply by injecting liquid fuel into air that has been compressed in the cylinder to a very high pressure (of the order of 700 pounds per square inch), and as a result of this compressing heated to a very high temperature (of the order of $1,500^\circ$ Fahrenheit). In a gasoline system, a fuel-injection system has a fairly easy job of it: the air stream into which the nozzles spray fuel is never much above or below the pressure of the outside air, and the temperature of the injector nozzle is never much above the temperature of boiling water. Also, although some fuel-injection gasoline engines have injector nozzles just upstream of each intake valve, the more common practice is to use only one nozzle at a central point (corresponding to the carburetor) for a four-cylinder engine, or two nozzles for an eight-cylinder engine.

Nothing about the fuel-injection system of a diesel engine can be called easy. The squirt of fuel causes combustion, so each cylinder must have its own injector nozzle, and it must deliver precisely the right amount of fuel (about the size of a pin's head) at precisely the right instant (as measured in millionths of a second) to accommodate the needs of the engine at the moment.

The diesel fuel-injection system consists of a **Fuel Supply Pump** (usually located inside the fuel tank), which delivers fuel to the engine compartment, a fine-grained **Fuel Filter** in the fuel line from the tank, a **Fuel-Metering Pump** a **Speed Governor**, and **Injection Nozzles** in each cylinder. Diesel engines are also equipped with **Glow Plugs** in each cylinder to provide the temperature boost that is needed to start a diesel engine at temperatures lower than about 65° Fahrenheit.

A diesel engine has no throttle valve of the kind illustrated on page 69; it runs "unthrottled," or at the equivalent of "full throttle," all the time: the cylinders suck in all the air the unobstructed intake-air passages can supply. Engine speed is controlled exclusively by the rate and the timing of fuel injection. Since the diesel engine has no electrical ignition system, you can't stop the engine by "turning off the ignition," but only by halting the flow of fuel to the cylinders. Like the fuel-injection gasoline engine, the diesel engine has no choke valve, and so the fuel-enriching that must be done to start a cold engine must be provided by the control apparatus on the metering pump. The speed governor is a crucial part of the control apparatus; it compares engine speed with the position of the accelerator pedal and causes the metering pump to increase or decrease the fuel feed rate as appropriate. As recently as the mid- or even late-Seventies diesel engines used injection-control systems that were largely mechanical and electromagnetic. More recently, micro-computer control has become prevalent.

Excessive fuel feed is the most likely cause of *black smoke* in diesel exhaust. Excessive fuel-injection rates may be the result of malfunctioning of the system, but it may result from excessive zeal on the part of a mechanic to get maximum "pep" out of the engine. Excessive fuel-injection rates do not cause *diesel stink*, but they can aggravate it. The characteristic unpleasant diesel-exhaust odor is caused by both incomplete combustion of the fuel and molecular rearrangement and partial oxidation of the hydrocarbon molecules at the high combustion temperatures that prevail in diesel engines. (Formaldehyde, which has a notably unpleasant odor, is one of the products of these chemical reactions.) Even a perfectly adjusted diesel engine puts out some diesel stink, but an imperfectly adjusted engine puts out more.

Since a diesel engine has no throttle valve, it does not "pull a vacuum" at any point in its system. Vacuum-operated apparatus such as power brakes, automatic transmission, and heater and air-conditioner controls are usually connected to the intake manifold of a gasoline engine, at a point downstream of the throttle plate. The intake manifold serves as the source of vacuum. In a diesel system, a separate **Vacuum Pump,** belt-driven by the engine, provides vacuum to operate the auxiliary devices.

Some engines, both gasoline and diesel, are equipped with **Turbochargers** to increase engine power. A turbocharger is an air blower, interposed between the air filter and the carburetor (or just upstream of the intake manifold if there is no carburetor.) It increases the volume of air that goes through the cylinders; and since the amount of fuel is increased correspondingly to maintain the desired fuel-to-air ratio, the effect of the turbocharger is to cause the engine to have the power output of a larger engine, without actually increasing the engine's physical size or its weight. The turbocharger fan is driven by exhaust gas on its way from the exhaust manifold to the downstream exhaust system. A damper valve called a **Wastegate** regulates the speed of the blower: when the pressure in the intake manifold exceeds the desired value, the damper valve causes part of the exhaust gas to bypass the turbocharger and go directly to the exhaust system.

## THE EXHAUST SYSTEM

An internal-combustion engine, be it gasoline- or diesel-fueled, equipped with carburetor or fuel-injection system, with or without turbocharger, generates power by causing hydrocarbon fuel (gasoline or diesel fuel) to burn rapidly in air. Air consists of approximately 20 percent oxygen and 80 percent nitrogen, and the fuel, whether gasoline or diesel fuel, consists predominantly of carbon and hydrogen. Ideally, when hydrocarbon fuel burns in air, the combustion products are harmless and unobjectionable: carbon plus oxygen yields **carbon dioxide,** and hydrogen plus oxygen yields water (in the form of steam at combustion temperatures). In practice, however, the combustion of fuel and air does not proceed ideally. It occurs very rapidly, at very high temperatures, at non-ideal proportions of oxygen and fuel and far less than ideal uniformity of mixing of fuel and air. In consequence, (a) not all of the fuel burns, and so there is an appreciable amount of unburned hydrocarbons in the gas that the cylinders discharge after combustion occurs, and in the case of diesel engines particularly, unburned fuel sometimes takes the form of **particulate matter**—i.e., microscopically small particles of unburned carbon, which form **black smoke,** (b) the combustion product contains a high proportion of **carbon monoxide** rather than carbon dioxide (and carbon monoxide is highly poisonous), and also (c) at the very high combustion temperatures, a small but by no means negligible fraction of the nitrogen in the combustion air combines chemically with the oxygen of the combustion air to form **nitrous oxides,** which are also poisonous and highly corrosive. In addition, most hydrocarbon fuels contain very small (but by no means negligible) concentrations of sulfur compounds, and in the combustion process these yield **sulfur dioxide,** another poisonous, corrosive gas. The **emission control** systems of modern automobiles are intended to combat these aberrant products of combustion.

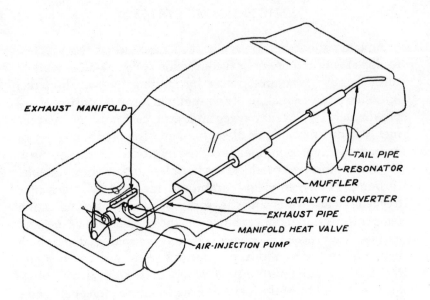

EXHAUST MANIFOLD

TAIL PIPE
RESONATOR
MUFFLER
CATALYTIC CONVERTER
EXHAUST PIPE
MANIFOLD HEAT VALVE
AIR-INJECTION PUMP

## Exhaust System

Overall, the exhaust system conducts the combustion products away from the engine and on to the outside air, and muffles the noise of the explosions. The simplest exhaust system consists of an *exhaust manifold* to collect the exhaust gases from all the cylinders into a single stream, an *exhaust pipe,* a *muffler,* and a *tail pipe.* Most exhaust systems also include a *manifold heat valve:* and if the engine is large, a second, smaller muffler called a *resonator* follows the main muffler, just ahead of the exhaust pipe. Most cars also have an *air-injection system* that reduces the concentrations of unburned fuel and carbon monoxide in the exhaust gas, and also a catalytic converter to complete the after-combustion process that the air injector initiates in the exhaust manifold. Some exhaust systems include a second catalytic converter that converts nitrous oxides back to harmless nitrogen and oxygen.

An important *WARNING* about leakage in the exhaust system is included among symptoms of malfunctions.

The **Exhaust Manifold** is a heavy steel pipe that is bolted onto the cylinder head of the engine to provide passageways for exhaust gases to flow from the exhaust valves of the individual cylinders into a common stream. V-8 engines have an exhaust manifold on each bank of cylinders. In an exhaust system that is equipped with an air-injection system, the exhaust manifold has holes opposite each cylinder outlet to accommodate air tubes (see discussion of air-injection, below). The exhaust manifold requires no maintenance, and it usually lasts as long as the rest of the car.

In an **Air Injection Reactor System** a special air pump provides a supply of compressed air, and this air is fed into the exhaust manifold at each point where exhaust gas leaves a cylinder through an exhaust valve. This air mixes with the hot exhaust gas at each point and causes further combustion of carbon monoxide, partially-burned gasoline, and unburned gasoline in the exhaust gas. The pump is driven by the engine by means of a belt, and a control valve in the system regulates the air injection to provide smooth operation. The system should be inspected every 15,000 miles for condition of belts and hoses, and to test the control valve for proper operation.

The air-injection system introduces surplus air into the exhaust manifold, to achieve more complete combustion. **Stratified-charge engines** also use surplus air for the same reason, but cause the further combustion to occur inside the cylinders rather than in the exhaust manifold and, later, the catalytic converter. Fuel-injection gasoline engines designed for stratified-charge operation inject liquid gasoline in the immediate neighborhood of the spark plugs. Combustion starts there and then spreads through the entire charge of air below in the cylinder. In other engines, one set of intake valves admits a high fuel-air mixture into the neighborhood of the spark plugs, and a second set of valves admits additional air lower down in the combustion chamber.

A **manifold heat valve** is used on gasoline engines to hasten the warming-up of the intake manifold when the engine is cold, and thus combat stalling. It is a thermostatically activated damper valve located between the exhaust manifold and the exhaust pipe. When the engine is cold the valve blocks the duct the exhaust gas normally flows through, and forces it to make a detour through passages in the engine intake manifold. As the engine warms up the thermostat turns the damper to the "straight-through" position and permits the exhaust gas to travel straight on to the exhaust pipe in the normal manner. In older cars, the thermostatic valve responds to the temperature of the exhaust gas; in recent models, it responds to the temperature of the coolant and actuates a vacuum diaphragm that in turn controls the damper valve.

The manifold heat valve should be checked every 5,000 miles to confirm that it still turns freely, and to lubricate it if necessary.

The **Exhaust Pipe** conducts exhaust gas from the exhaust manifold, or from the manifold heat valve unit, to the muffler. If the car has a V-8 engine and a dual exhaust system, an exhaust pipe is provided for each bank of cylinders; the remainder of the exhaust system, all the way back to the tail pipes, is also done in duplicate and there is no interconnection between the two assemblies. The more conventional arrangement is to have a Y-shaped exhaust pipe that connects onto both manifolds at the front end and, at the back end, connects onto the muffler.

The ratio of fuel to air in the cylinders is a critical factor in achieving optimum performance and economy in an internal-combustion engine. The *oxygen content of the exhaust gas* can be used as a measure of fuel-to-air ratio, and modern microprocessors can use this information, along with other information, to *control* the rate of fuel feed to the engine. An **oxygen sensor** feeds oxygen-content information to the microprocessor.

If your car has a **Catalytic Converter**, it is located at the rear of the exhaust pipe, ahead of the muffler. It may have *two* catalytic converter units.

A catalytic converter is a cylindrical or oval tank to which exhaust pipes are connected fore and aft. Inside is a bed of granular material impregnated with one or more "catalysts," which are chemical compounds that promote specific chemical reactions without themselves being affected. One group of catalysts promotes the combustion of any carbon monoxide or unburned fuel that may be in the exhaust gas with any free oxygen that may be present. A second kind of catalyst promotes the decomposition of nitrous oxides back to nitrogen and oxygen. Cars of the mid-Seventies have a single catalytic converter containing combustion catalyst; it reinforces the air-injection system, the purpose of which is to add additional air, hence free oxygen, to the exhaust gas. This original type of catalyst has no effect on nitrogen oxides in the exhaust; some later models therefore employed a second catalytic converter containing the decomposition catalyst. Some still-more-recent models use a newer **three way catalyst,** which is capable of performing both the combustion and decomposing functions.

Cars with diesel engines or stratified-charge engines usually do not require catalytic converters because their exhaust contains very little unburned fuel.

It should be noted that a failure of your catalytic converter can keep your car from starting. Normally, the catalytic converter will last 40,000 miles without any problem.

**Leaded gasoline** must not be used in an engine that is equipped with a catalytic converter because combustion products containing lead compounds "poison" the combustion catalyst—that is, they render the catalyst ineffective. Leaded gasoline contains **tetraethyl lead** to reduce spark knock (see page 105). Unleaded gasoline consists of hydrocarbon molecules that have more favorable burning characteristics and therefore do not require anti-knock additives.

By its very nature a catalytic converter is a **fire hazard** of a particular kind. Its function is to cause unburned gasoline and carbon monoxide to burn up; and since such burning generates a lot of heat, the catalytic converter becomes very hot. If you park your car on grass you may destroy the grass; and if the grass is dry to begin with, you may start a grass fire—underneath your car!

In some circumstances a catalytic converter will cause exhaust gases to have a rotten-egg odor. Sulfur in the gasoline is responsible for the stink. You may have bought gasoline that contains excessive sulfur. A second possibility is that the fuel mixture going to the engine is too rich; hence the normal (very low) concentration of sulfur in the gasoline is high enough in the exhaust gas to cause the rotten-egg smell.

The catalyst used in catalytic converters is designed to last for 50,000 miles. Some catalytic converters can be recharged with new catalyst; others must be replaced with a new unit.

The **Muffler** is a cylindrical tank inside of which are pipes and partitions with holes drilled in them. The muffler breaks up the pressure waves of the exhaust gases which issue from the exhaust valves of the engine cylinders in explosive bursts. The results of breaking up the pressure waves is to smooth out the pop-pop-pop of the explosions and convert it to a smooth purrrrrrrrr

A **Resonator** is an undersized muffler that is often added to the exhaust system of a large engine to further muffle the noise that gets through the main muffler. The smaller muffler is called by a different name simply to avoid confusion.

The life expectancy of mufflers is discussed in the section below entitled Life Expenctancy of Mufflers and Pipes.

The **Tail Pipe** is the rearmost pipe in the exhaust system. If the system includes more than one muffler and-or a catalytic converter, then one or more **Intermediate Pipes** are also included in the system. Like the exhaust pipe and the muffler(s), these additional pipes must be replaced when they rust through. If any of the pipes should get flattened or distorted (as by backing into a high curb, for example) it should be repaired promptly. Engine performance suffers greatly if the flow of exhaust gas is impeded. Flow restrictions also greatly increase the exhaust gas hazard that is described in the Problems chapter. A restriction increases the pressure in the exhaust system, and thus increases the probability of leakage into the car.

**Life Expectancy of Mufflers and Pipes** varies widely, depending upon both the service the automobile is in and the local weather and road conditions. The major enemy of mufflers and related piping is rust on both the inside and the outside. Water is a primary product of the combustion of any motor fuel. This water is present in exhaust gas in the form of steam, but when the exhaust gas goes into a cold system of piping and mufflers the steam condenses to water which lies inside as a puddle until it evaporates away. If you use your car mostly for very short trips, the rearmost parts of the exhaust system may never be free of water lying in low spots, rusting the metal inside.

Road puddles attack the exhaust system from the outside; and so a rainy climate is harder on exhaust systems than a dry climate; and salt applied to roads to combat ice and snow in winter, or sprayed into air by nature in seaside communities, makes a serious problem much more serious.

The exhaust manifold in your automobile is a heavy steel casting, and it is not likely to rust through during the lifetime of the car, although it may crack, because of stresses in the manufacturing process or some mishap in its career.

The exhaust pipe is usually made of reasonably heavy-gauge steel, and it is likely to outlast several mufflers and tail pipes— especially since the exhaust pipe provides no low spots where water can collect.

## THE COOLING SYSTEM

The cooling system keeps the engine temperature down to satisfactory operating levels by conducting heat away from cylinders. Combustion of the fuel mixture in the cylinders generates temperatures of the order of 5000°F, and if the heat were not conducted away the engine would very soon stop running because of overheating, and be damaged, perhaps beyond repair.

A few cars, most notably the Volkswagen "Beetle" of yesteryear, use an **air cooling system.** A large fan blasts a stream of air over the cylinders to cool them, and that's all there is to it. Air cooling imposes serious design limitations and has other shortcomings, but it is a simple system and little can go wrong with it.

In most cars the engine is cooled by circulating a liquid coolant through a network of spaces in the engine block and cylinder head, surrounding the cylinders. This network is called the *water jacket.* The coolant flowing through the water jacket absorbs heat from the engine, thereby cooling the engine; in the process, however, the coolant itself becomes hot and is no longer able to cool the engine and must be replaced by a cooler liquid. This is done by pumping the coolant that has just become heated through the *radiator*, where it is cooled by a flow of air. It is replaced in the water jacket by coolant that has just come from the radiator. Thus, this closed system consists essentially of a quantity of liquid which flows around and around, from engine to radiator and back to engine, being first heated, then cooled, then heated, then cooled. The other important parts of the system are a *water pump, hoses,* a *thermostat* to control the temperature of the coolant, and an electric or belt-driven *fan* to blast air over the radiator. The heater-defroster inside the car is also connected into the cooling system; whenever either of these is turned on, part of the hot coolant is diverted to the heater or defroster instead of the radiator. The next sketch shows the arrangement of components in a typical cooling system. On the instrument panel of the car, connected with the cooling system, is either a *temperature gauge* to report the temperature of the coolant, or an *alarm light* to tell you when the coolant is too hot.

The **Coolant** used in a liquid-cooling system is a mixture of water and **ethylene glycol antifreeze.** Ethylene glycol both lowers the freezing point and raises the boiling point of water. Water freezes at 32 degrees Fahrenheit and boils (at sea level) at 212 degrees, whereas a mixture of equal parts of water and ethylene glycol freezes at −34 degrees and boils at about 235 degrees. The

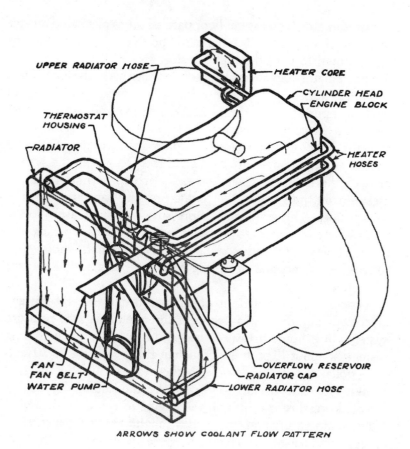

ARROWS SHOW COOLANT FLOW PATTERN

## The Cooling System

life-expectancy of ethylene glycol is about two years. If it is kept
in service too long, it is oxidized to a corrosive acidic material,
oxalic acid, that attacks aluminum parts of engines and cooling
systems with particular severity.

It is essential that coolant circulate in order to cool the engine.
If circulation stops for any reason, including the freezing of the
coolant in winter, the coolant that happens to be in the water
jacket will soon become very hot and be converted to steam,
which will soon force its way out of the *radiator cap.*

The **Radiator** is an assembly of parallel tubes of small diameter through which coolant is circulated and over which a stream of air is blown to cool the liquid inside.

The **Radiator Cap** covers the radiator filler neck, through which coolant is added to the system, but it also serves a second and equally important function. The radiator cap is the pressure-relief valve for the cooling system. The cooling system operates at a pressure of about 15 pounds per square inch, roughly the same as that of a home pressure cooker. If the pressure in the system exceeds the intended level, the radiator cap permits steam to escape from the system, just as the pressure cap on a pressure cooker does. This prevents the pressure from increasing to the point where it would blow hose connections loose, or actually rupture hoses. If the radiator cap is faulty, it permits water vapor to leak out at normal operating pressures, and so the coolant evaporates away.

A coolant mixture made up of equal parts of water and ethylene glycol boils at about 235 degrees Fahrenheit in a zero-pressure system. In a home pressure cooker or an automobile cooling system, at about 15 pounds per inch in either case, the 50:50 mixture boils about 30 degrees higher, at about 265 degrees Fahrenheit. One reason for operating the cooling system at elevated pressure is to permit the engine to run at a somewhat higher temperature and thus achieve slightly better fuel efficiency. A second reason, which may be more important than the first, is to enable the car manufacturer to equip the car with a considerably smaller and less expensive radiator.

Any leak in the cooling system will permit coolant or steam to squirt out rapidly, and the engine will soon overheat for lack of coolant. If you should be confronted with a **cooling system emergency** caused by a leak, you may be able to limp home by operating the cooling system under zero pressure instead of elevated pressure. After letting the system cool down to the point where you can remove the radiator cap safely, simply fill the radiator with water and drive with the radiator cap only loosely in place, rather than tightly shut. Leakage will be very much less rapid at zero pressure. You should of course check the radiator level every few miles and add water as needed. If the cap is not tightly clamped down and the cooling system is not under pressure, it is not necessary to cool the system down before removing the radiator cap unless the cap is actually steaming.

Many cooling systems have a **Radiator Overflow Reservoir** connected to the radiator filler neck. The purpose of this reservoir is to prevent the exposure of hot coolant to air, since air oxidizes ethylene glycol to corrosive oxalic acid (mentioned earlier) much more rapidly at elevated temperatures than at air temperature. The reservoir is partly filled with coolant. As the engine warms up, the coolant in the cooling system expands and overflows through the radiator cap into the reservoir. Later, when the engine is shut down and cools off, the coolant in the system contracts and sucks part of the coolant in the reservoir back into the radiator. Thus, the cooling system is always completely filled with liquid, and the coolant is ever exposed to air at radiator temperatures.

If your car does not have an overflow reservoir, your mechanic can install one at modest cost.

**Radiator Hoses** connect the top of the engine water jacket to the top of the radiator and the bottom of the radiator with the water (i.e., the coolant) pump which is bolted onto the front of the engine. **Heater Hoses** connect the heater-defroster unit inside the car into the cooling system. One hose leads from the top of the engine to a heater connection at the rear of the engine compartment. A second hose leads from a nearby heater connection back to the water pump. Failure of radiator hoses is often sudden and may be so serious that you cannot even limp home at zero pressure (as discussed above). Radiator and heater hoses should be inspected at 5,000-mile intervals, and replaced every 25,000 miles—even though they might last considerably longer. The extra cost of premature replacement is inexpensive insurance against inconvenient and costly failure.

The **Fan** sucks air through the radiator, to promote cooling of the liquid in the cooling system. In many cars the fan is driven by an electric motor which is turned on and off by a switch which in turn is actuated by a **coolant temperature sensor**. Such fans operate entirely independently of the engine; they often continue to run for several minutes after the engine is shut down, because the coolant temperature is above the "switch-on" point.

Other cars use mechanically driven fans, which are attached to the pulley on the water pump (see below) that is belt-driven by a pulley on the front of the engine. (What is sometimes referred to as the **fan belt** is primarily and more importantly the *water-pump belt*; its maintenance is discussed below.) Some mechanical systems incorporate a **fan clutch** that automatically frees the fan from its drive shaft when the air in the engine compartment is cold and no help is needed to cool the liquid in the radiator. The clutch also disengages when the fan speed exceeds a predetermined level, since at high speeds the rush of air through the radiator provides sufficient cooling, and no help from the fan is needed.

The fan clutch has high but indefinite life-expectance. If the engine overheats abnormally at low speeds in hot weather, be suspicious of the fan clutch first of all. Precautionary replacement of the fan clutch at 75,000-mile intervals is justifiable as relatively inexpensive insurance against cooling-system problems at hundred-degree temperatures in crawling traffic.

The **Water Pump** circulates coolant through the water jacket of the engine and the radiator, and thus causes heat to be conducted away from the engine to the air that cools the radiator. The engine will overheat to the point of incipient damage in just a few minutes if circulation of coolant is halted. The **water pump belt** that drives the water pump should be inspected for tautness every 5,000 miles, and replaced (even though it might serve longer) every 25,000 miles as a preventive measure. The life expectancy of the water pump itself is of the order of 75,000-100,000 miles. Leakage is the most common symptom of failure, but sometimes the pump gives preliminary warning by emitting a penetrating squeal when the engine is running.

If a fan is attached to the water pump and the fan is loose and "wiggles" this can be a sign of a bad water pump.

The water pump requires better lubrication than water alone can provide. Ethylene glycol in the coolant serves as a lubricant. In an emergency, you can operate the car for a hundred miles or so with water alone as the coolant, but even this will shorten the life expectancy of the water seal in the pump.

A car with an independent electrically-driven fan can be operated safely with a leaky water pump, provided water is added frequently enough to keep the temperature down. (The radiator cap should be only loosely in place, so the cooling system is at zero pressure and leakage is minimized.) If the fan is mounted on the water-pump pulley, there is some risk that the fan will pull loose and damage the radiator. In an emergency, the fan can be unbolted from the pulley, and you may be able to limp home—adding water frequently to counteract overheating.

> **Cold water might crack a very hot engine!**
> Do not add water to a steaming radiator. If it has been steam-ing *vigorously,* stop the engine for at least 30 minutes; then add water *slowly.*

The **Thermostat** is located at the top forward end of the engine, just ahead of the point where the top radiator hose is attached to the engine. The thermostat is a valve that controls the flow of coolant from the water jacket to the radiator in order to help the engine warm up. When a cold engine first starts up, the coolant is prevented by the thermostat valve from circulating in its usual brisk manner. When the engine and the coolant have warmed up to an appropriate temperature, the thermostat valve opens and permits the coolant to circulate.

A thermostat can fail either by failing to open or failing to close. The first kind of failure is less likely, but more troublesome, because it makes itself known by causing the engine to overheat: that is, the coolant is prevented from circulating by the closed thermostat valve even after the engine has warmed up. The se-cond kind of failure—that of a failure of the valve to close when the engine is cold—may escape your notice if you have only an alarm light rather than a temperature gauge on your instrument panel. A temperature gauge will give you persistently low readings if the thermostat valve is not closing when it should.

After an overheating condition, if the hose leading to the housing is cooler than the coolant hoses, the thermostat is closed when it should be open.

The life expectancy of a thermostat is about 75,000—100,000 miles. To avoid **a failure** it is wise to replace the thermostat and water pump at 75,000 miles.

The cooling system has a **Sending Unit** located in the water jacket that actuates either a **Water Temperature Gauge** or an **Alarm Light** on the instrument panel. Generally speaking, a temperature gauge is designed to read somewhere near mid-scale when the engine is at normal operating temperature, but this is not invariably so. The temperature will run noticeably higher at high speeds than at low speeds, higher in hot weather than in cold, higher when climbing a long grade, and higher when the air-conditioning system is on than when it is not. (The air-conditioner puts an additional load on the engine, just as hill-climbing does; in either case, the greater load causes the engine to run hotter.) The engine temperature will also tend to run high in very slow traffic in very hot weather. This is because some of the air going through the radiator is normally sucked in by the forward motion of the car; when the car is traveling very slowly, the fan must do all the work, and if the weather is very hot, this may not be sufficient.

---

### Important Note
### about the Red Temperature Light

This light is supposed to flash red when you turn the key to the "Start" position, and then go off when the engine starts. If it fails to flash on, this means the bulb is burned out. Have the bulb replaced right away. An alarm light that doesn't work is worse than useless.

An **Engine Temperature Alarm Light** glows red when the sending unit indicates that the coolant is too hot. Some cars have an additional light that glows blue or green when the engine is underheated; as soon as the engine comes up to a normal operating range this light goes off. The "cold" light is not as important as the "hot" light; but if it persists in staying on, it is telling you that the thermostat is stuck in the open position. Bear in mind, however, that the temperature alarm system might give a false alarm. Investigate immediately, of course; but if there is no steam, and if the engine runs no more noisily than usual, you may confidently—but cautiously and attentively—proceed on your way.

**Cooling System Leaks.** Ideally, you would put a fresh charge of coolant into your cooling system every other October, say, and never give it another thought. Unfortunately, this is not an ideal world. In the real world, cooling systems develop leaks. You should have the level of your coolant checked once a month or so, in the course of gasoline stops, and water added as it is needed. If you have to add more than half a pint or so of water a month, you probably have a leak somewhere in the system, and you should have your mechanic find the leak and correct it.

There are several possibilities. If the radiator cap does not seal tightly it permits water vapor to escape at normal operating temperatures and pressures. A radiator hose or heater hose may be leaking where it is connected onto the radiator or engine or heater unit, or the hose itself may have developed a crack or split. The radiator or the heater core inside the car may be leaking. The water pump seal may have developed a leak. **Freeze plugs** protect the water jacket; one of these may have developed a leak. A very slight leak may have developed between the cylinder head and the engine block, which permits combustion gases to leak into the water jacket and force coolant out through the radiator overflow pipe.

Some cooling system leaks leave evidence you can detect; wet spots on the pavement, or steam, or spewing liquid. (Air-conditioning units in normal operation drip water to the ground at the right side of the car just forward of the front door; do not interpret a wet spot here as a cooling-system leak if the air-conditioner has been running.) A wet carpet in the passenger compartment may indicate a heater-defroster leak.

Other leaks do not leave evidence. A faulty radiator cap permits water vapor to escape without leaving a trace. A hose connection may leak only when the cooling system is under pressure and the liquid may drip onto a hot surface and evaporate: again, no trace.

Cooling-system leaks cannot be tolerated. If the problem is something other than a badly ruptured hose, it is usually possible to limp home, but prompt repair is essential if the car is to be satisfactory in normal everyday service. All of the components are repairable or replaceable at modest cost. Furthermore, repairs to the cooling system should be of first quality. Anti-leak additives stocked by most filling stations are not a permanent cure. They are touted on the label as effective in repairing leaks in cooling systems, and while they may get you home—perhaps even over considerable distances in some situations—they are no substitute for the repairing or replacing of faulty parts.

## THE CHARGING SYSTEM

The charging system generates electrical energy and stores it for use as needed by the starter, the ignition system, the lights, the instruments, and all the other apparatus and equipment that is driven by or otherwise uses electrical energy. The charging system consists of an *alternator* (sometime called a *generator)*, a *voltage regulator*, a *battery*, and either an *ammeter* or a *warning light*. The sketch below shows the arrangement of these parts. The word "ground" in the sketch means the car frame or any metal part directly attached to the frame, as for example the engine, the body, or the bumpers.

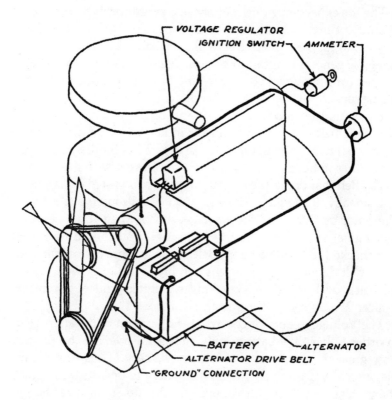

*Charging System*

The **Alternator**, or **Generator**, located to one side at the front of the engine, is driven by the engine by means of a belt, usually the fan belt; the belt forces the alternator to rotate, and thus supplies mechanical energy; the alternator transforms this mechanical energy to electrical energy. The heavier the demand on the generating system for electrical current, the greater the resistance of the alternator to the belt drive, and the greater the mechanical load on the engine. It is for this reason that your gasoline mileage is lower when you use the headlights, for example, or the heater, or the air conditioner, or any other electrical apparatus: the engine can supply more power only by using more gasoline.

The life expectancy of the alternator is ordinarily of the order of 50,000 miles, but this does not appear to be true for all makes and vintages. Your mechanic will probably be able to tell you what the general reputation of your make is. Alternator failure is often foreshadowed by a squealing or tapping noise when the engine runs, or by persistent undercharging of the battery. (Undercharging may turn out to be the fault of the voltage regulator, described below.) Actual failure is indicated by an alarm light or ammeter. If your alternator lasts for 50,000 miles it is prudent either to have it overhauled or to replace it with a new one.

The **Belt** that drives the alternator must be adjusted for tautness occasionally; it should be checked at 5,000-mile intervals. A loose alternator belt often produces a harsh squeal when you accelerate the engine; so if you have this symptom, you should have the belt checked reasonably soon. Belt slippage aggravates wear and other belt damage, and shortens belt life. The life expectancy of the belt is of the order of 35,000 miles, but it is prudent to replace it after 25,000 miles to forestall failure.

The **Voltage Regulator** controls the operation of the alternator in order to keep the battery fully charged if possible, no matter how great the electrical drain on the battery. Thus, for example, after you draw energy from the battery to operate the starter, the voltage regulator "turns the alternator up" to restore energy to the battery as rapidly as the alternator is capable of supplying it; as soon as the battery is fully charged, the regulator "turns the alternator down."

The life expectancy of the voltage regulator is high: it is customary to replace the regulator whenever the alternator is overhauled or replaced.

An **Ammeter** (a gauge) or a **Warning Light** on the instrument panel reports on the operation of the charging system. The indicator, whether gauge or light, may be labeled "Gen," or "Alt," or "Bat," or "Charge." A *gauge* should point to the "charge" (or "plus" or "+") side of the scale when the engine runs faster than the equivalent of about 10 miles per hour, but at idling speed it may normally point to the left or "discharge" (or "minus" or "−") side of the scale. For a brief period after the starter has been operated, the gauge should indicate a substantial rate of charge, but it is normal for it then to fall back to a fairly low level after the battery has been restored to full charge.

A *warning light* is normally turned off when the engine is running, but it may glow faintly when the engine is idling without signifying trouble. If the light goes on when the engine is running at substantially greater than idling speed, however, it tells you that the alternator is not doing its job: it is supplying current at a lower rate than the current is being used. Also, the warning light is supposed to turn on when you turn the ignition key to "On," but before you turn the key further, to "Start." If the light does *not* go on prior to start-up, it means the bulb has burned out or something else has failed in the alarm system. You should have it checked right away.

Some cars are equipped with a **voltmeter** on the instrument panel, instead of or in addition to an ammeter or warning light. A very inexpensive alternative to the factory-installed voltmeter is now available in retail electronics shops under the name **electrical system analyzer** or words to that effect.

The voltmeter indicates the voltage of the car's electrical system at the moment. For most car owners the moment of greatest interest and value is the moment of "steady operation" after the engine has warmed up and when the car is running at 10-40 miles per hour. In these circumstances the voltage should be 14.0 to 15.2 volts—nearer the lower end of the range in warm weather, and nearer the upper than the lower end in cold weather. (Voltages outside the range by 0.5 volt in very hot weather or very cold weather are not unusual and not alarming.)

The electrical system analyzer is an inexpensive electronic voltmeter that has (usually) three lights, one of which flashes on if the voltage is in the normal range, another if it is outside on the low side, and the third if it is outside the range on the high side. The instrument is simply plugged into a cigarette-lighter socket to connect it into the electrical system.

A mechanic or sophisticated near-mechanic can derive quite a bit of useful information from the precise voltage of the system under wide-ranging circumstances. But even on a mundane level, electrical-system voltage can often provide advance warning of trouble in the making, and you don't have to be a mechanic to realize the you would be prudent to have the charging system checked promptly. If under the "steady operation" conditions described above the system voltage is outside the normal range, then either the voltage regulator needs adjusting or the battery, regulator, or alternator is malfunctioning. It is better to act on suspicion than to find out later that you weren't anxious *enough.*

Failure of the alternator to generate current does not require immediate shut-down. For as long as the battery will supply the electrical energy needed to operate the car you may continue; nothing would be damaged by continuing until it stops. A fully charged battery in good condition can supply the electrical needs of the ignition system for many dozens of miles; but if the headlights or heater/air conditioner blower are on, or if the starter is operated, the battery will run down much sooner.

The **Battery** is a storage reservoir for electrical energy generated by the alternator. It works by means of a chemical interaction between *plates* made of lead and plates made of lead oxide, all immersed in a liquid mixture of sulfuric acid and water that is called *battery acid* or *electrolyte.* The battery has six *cells*—that is, six separate reservoirs of electrolyte in which are located assemblies of battery plates. Each cell generates two volts, so the overall voltage of the battery is six times two, or twelve, volts. Some batteries have removable caps, one on each cell, to facilitate checking for electrolyte level. Other batteries are "sealed": the cover plates over the cells must be pried off to inspect electrolyte levels.

In service, water evaporates from the electrolyte and causes the electrolyte level to drop. It is essential that the electrolyte level be higher than the tops of the plates, and so water must be added from time to time. Generally speaking, batteries with removable caps require water more frequently than "sealed" batteries, but even the latter should be checked at 5,000-mile intervals.

**Battery gas is explosive! Never bring an open flame to within a yard of a car battery!**

The inter-relationship of alternator, voltage regulator, and battery is the cause of much mis-diagnosis of ailments in this department. Many is the perfectly sound battery that has been junked because the owner thought it was dead, when in fact the fault lay not in the battery but in the charging apparatus—the alternator or the voltage regulator. Both of these should be checked before replacing the battery, unless the battery has obviously served its time.

Another familiar false alarm is caused by the formation of a deposit between the battery posts and the battery cable connectors. This deposit interferes with the flow of current. Battery posts and cable connectors should be cleaned routinely every 10,000 miles to combat this problem.

A third false alarm is caused by the low electrolyte level in one or more cells of the battery. Current output by the battery depends upon contact between electrolyte and plate surfaces; if the electrolyte level is too low, then the contact area is smaller than it should be and the current output is correspondingly reduced. In addition, the plates will be damaged if they are allowed to dry out excessively. Electrolyte level should be checked no less frequently than once a month, and water added if it is needed to restore the level. (Sealed batteries do not permit this attention, of course.) Distilled water or de-ionized water is preferable to kitchen-sink water because the latter contains dissolved minerals that gradually foul the plate surfaces. No more than about 8 ounces of water a month should be required to keep the electrolyte level in all six cells up to normal. If your battery requires more than this, it probably means that the voltage regulator is out of adjustment on the high side and should be checked.

Ultimately, of course, your battery will die. If you are lucky you will be forewarned that the end is near and you will recognize the warning: the battery doesn't seem to be very peppy even after a long drive; or it seems to "run down" if the car sits for a few days; or it does not seem to be capable of delivering current in the amount the starter requires. If in checking the battery your mechanic discovers marked differences in the state of charge of two or more cells—with one cell showing a one-half charge, say, when the other cells show full charge; or one-fourth charge as compared with three-fourths charge for the others—you should then replace the battery, because total failure is not far away.

Virtually all automobile batteries are "warranted" for specific periods of service, and modern quality-control techniques enable manufacturers to match warranty and actual lifetime of the battery fairly well. In order to collect on a battery warranty, however, you must deliver to the dealer a battery that has actually *failed*—that has actually shut you down; and the warranty is usually null and void if the battery case has cracked, or a battery post has worked loose, or any deterioration is observable other than a simple failure to accept and hold a charge. You may be wise to simply replace the battery as a preventive measure at the first genuine suspicion of trouble, without regard for any warranty period that may still apply. Choosing your own time, you may be able to buy a battery at a better price without any "adjustment" than you would have to pay after adjustment in an emergency.

**Battery Charging** can be done by any filling station: in a period of 30 minutes to an hour a run-down battery can be brought up to full charge—or to as much of a charge as it will take. If you live in a severe climate and your car must live outside night and day, you may wish to buy a **Battery Booster,** or **Trickle Charger,** for the dual purpose of keeping your battery at least slightly warm by passing a small charging current through it overnight, and adding to the total charge of the battery. Your mechanic will be able to advise you on this.

## THE IGNITION SYSTEM

Gasoline engines require an ignition system to supply a spark at precisely the right instant in each cylinder to ignite the gasoline-air mixture in that cylinder. Diesel engines do not require an ignition system: as discussed in the Fuel System chapter, combustion occurs spontaneously when liquid diesel fuel is squirted into air that has been compressed to a very high pressure, and thus heated to a very high temperature, in a cylinder.

The basic parts of the ignition system are a *battery* to supply the electrical energy, an *ignition switch*, a combination of an *ignition coil* (sometimes called a *spark coil*) and *current interrupter* to generate a high voltage from the current supplied by the battery, a *distributor* (consisting primarily of a *rotor* and a *distributor cap*), a *spark plug* for each cylinder, and a *spark plug lead* (or "cable") to conduct current from the distributor to each of the spark plugs. The next sketch portrays the arrangement.

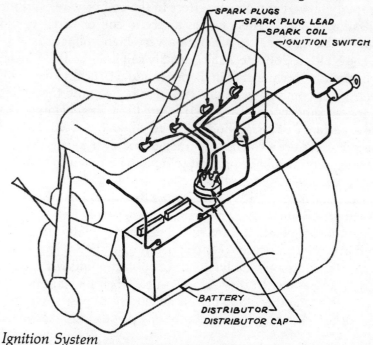

*Ignition System*

The **Ignition Switch** performs one simple function in the ignition system: it causes current to flow from the battery through the ignition coil, and thus to activate the ignition system.

The **Ignition Coil** and a current interrupter (described further below), acting together, amplify the voltage that is available from the battery (12-15 volts) approximately fifteen-hundred-fold (up to about 20,000 volts). The amplifier section of a radio or phonograph performs a similar function, although by an entirely different method. The voltages received by a radio from an antenna or by a phonograph from a pickup head are minute voltages; they must be amplified many thousand-fold to be strong enough to cause a loud speaker to emit sound. Similarly, the 12 to 15 volts available from a battery could not jump the gap of a spark plug, but a 20,000-volt current can.

The ignition system achieves its voltage amplification by interrupting the flow of current through a coil of wire, and thus converting the steady flow to pulses of current. These pulses cause a rapidly changing magnetic effect in the coil of wire; and the pulsating magnetic effect causes a second coil of wire, wound around the first one, to generate a very high voltage.

The **Ignition Coil** (mechanics usually call it **the coil**) is a metal cylinder about two inches in diameter and 6-8 inches long, with three wires coming out of one end. It is bolted onto the engine in the neighborhood of the distributor (described below). The life expectancy of an ignition coil is very high but it will not last forever; and since a coil usually (though not always) fails without warning, you would be prudent to replace it after 100,000 miles as a precautionary measure.

Most cars older than 1975 models use **Breaker Points** (also called **Distributor Points,** or, by most mechanics, simply **Points**) as the current-interrupter that converts the steady current to a pulsating current in the ignition coil. For convenience, the points are located in the distributor assembly: a pair of contact points that permit current to pass when they "close"—i.e., when they are in contact with each other—and permit no current to pass when they are "open." A cam in the distributor opens and closes the points.

When the engine runs at idling speed, the points open and close 10 to 30 times per second; at highway speeds, this "make-and-break" rate is of the order of 100 to 200 times a second. Each time the points open a slight spark jumps from one to the other, and each spark causes a minute amount of damage to the contact surfaces of the points. A **condenser,** also located inside the distributor assembly, is included in the circuit to serve as an electrical "cushion" that absorbs some of the energy of interruption, and thus reduces the amount of sparking. The distributor points should be checked every 5,000 miles for electrical resistance and cycle of opening and closing, and cleaned or adjusted, or both, if necessary.

Most cars newer than 1975 models use **Electronic Ignition** systems instead of breaker-point systems. Some electronic systems have make-and-break points, but they carry negligible currents and hence do not deteriorate appreciably in service; other systems use "non-contact" points that do not actually touch but only *approach* each other closely enough to set off effects in an associated electronic amplifier. This amplifier serves as the current-interrupter that causes the coil to generate its high voltage (which may be higher than breaker points can produce) in the usual manner. The performance of the electronic ignition system should be checked at 25,000-mile intervals. Generally speaking, the "electronic module" is not repairable—only replaceable.

The **Distributor** distributes the high-voltage current to each spark plug in turn at the instant a spark is needed to ignite the fuel mixture. This is achieved by having a rotor carry the current from a central contact inside the distributor cap to each of several contact points located in a circular path.

In some ignition systems the ignition coil is built into the distributor cap, to reduce the amount of external wiring that carries the very high voltage needed by the spark plugs.

The **Distributor Cap** is the crown-shaped plastic top that covers the distributor. A heavily insulated wire leads from the spark coil to the center of the cap; this carries the high-voltage current that the spark coil generates from the pulsating currents mentioned above. Around the outside of the top of the cap are sockets, and into each socket is plugged a heavily insulated wire that leads to a spark plug.

Inside the distributor, a wand-shaped **Rotor** rotates, and provides a path for the current from the center socket to each of the peripheral sockets. Thus does the distributor distribute the high-voltage current. The timing of this distribution, so that it occurs at precisely the right place at the right time, is discussed under *timing* later in this chapter.

Excessive water on either the outside or the inside of the distributor cap "kills the ignition" by providing a path for the current to leak away instead of going through the spark plugs. This problem sometimes arises in very rainy or humid weather when moisture condenses on cold surfaces. Usually the difficulty, if this is it, can be cured by drying the cap with a cloth. It is not always necessary to remove the cap and dry the inside, but occasionally it is.

Both the distributor cap and the rotor are exposed to extensive electrical sparking in their normal service, and in time they develop cracks and fissures through which current can leak. The cap also gradually becomes more susceptible to moisture as a result of this spark damage and it should be replaced routinely every 25,000 miles, or sooner if the car develops greater reluctance to start or if it stalls persistently in wet weather.

**Spark-Plug Leads,** sometimes called **Spark-Plug Cables,** are lengths of heavily insulated wire that conduct the high-voltage current from sockets in the distributor cap to each spark plug. The wire inside the insulation may be made of metal, but more often it is made of carbon since carbon-core cables cause less trouble with radio static than do metallic cables. Carbon-core cables are comparatively fragile, and a rough jerk on a cable can rupture the core and render the cable inoperative. The result is unsteady running of the engine because one of the cylinders, deprived of its spark, does not fire. The other thing that goes wrong with spark-plug leads is cracking or other deterioration of the insulation after long exposure to heat in the engine compartment. The result of this will be engine unsteadiness. Your mechanic will inspect spark-plug leads each time he inspects or replaces spark plugs. They do not have infinite life expectancy, however, and they should be replaced, as a precautionary measure, every 50,000 miles on engines with breaker point ignition. Engines with electronic ignition require much more expensive, but longer-lived, cables. These can be kept in service until, in routine periodic inspection, your mechanic discovers deterioration.

**Spark Plugs** provide the spark that ignites the fuel mixture in the cylinder—the final purpose of the ignition system. The most characteristic part of a spark plug is the white porcelain insulator that forms its main body. Inside the insulator is a metal rod that leads from the end of the insulator, where the spark-plug lead is connected, down into the combustion chamber of the cylinder. A second, shorter, rod is attached to the base of the plug, inside the combustion chamber. The tips of the two rods are located about 1/32 inch apart; the space between them is the "spark gap" across which the high-voltage current jumps to make the spark that ignites the fuel mixture in the cylinder. In a new plug the gap is about as wide as a dime is thick, but after the plug has been in service for 10,000 miles it is about as wide as a quarter is thick. The reason for this widening is that each spark removes a minute amount of metal—and at 50 miles per hour, for example, the sparking frequency is of the order of 20 times per second.

If your car has a breaker-point distributor, it is prudent to replace the spark plugs every 10,000 miles in the interests of good gasoline mileage. Engines of 1974 and later vintage vary widely in their spark-plug consumption. Plugs last 25,000 to 50,000 miles in some such engines, but in others they must be replaced after 10,000 miles at best. How to handle this: have your plugs inspected every 10,000 miles until you learn from experience how often they should be inspected and replaced. As a part of this exploration you should consult your mechanic about "hot" versus "intermediate" versus "cold" plugs. Spark plugs are available in several different "heat ranges;" an intermediate heat range is suitable for most cars and most usages. But if your car is used exclusively for short-trip, stop-and-go service, fouling of the spark plugs with oil and carbon might be a serious problem; "hot" plugs would do a better job of burning off the deposit. On long trips, the combustion chamber reaches and maintains very much higher temperatures than it does in short-trip service, and standard spark plugs may run hotter than necessary to do their job with the result that the electrodes are consumed more rapidly than necessary. In that case, "cold" plugs would be preferable.

**Timing** refers to the adjustment of the distributor that controls the exact time at which the spark occurs in the combustion chamber. The precise instant at which the spark should occur under standardized conditions of operation of the engine is carefully defined and published for each make and model of engine. Normally, the specifications call for the spark to jump when the piston is a few thousandths of an inch (carefully specified in terms of degrees of rotation of the crankshaft) before it reaches the top of its travel. Checking and adjusting the timing is a comparatively simple operation. It should be done routinely every 15,000 miles.

Most cars employ **microprocessors** to control ignition, and in most cases fuel feed as well. Sensors report to a specialized computer a wide array of information about engine speed, car speed, throttle setting, intake-manifold pressure, exhaust-gas oxygen content, coolant temperature, air temperature, and other factors (these vary from system to system). The computer (whether controlling a diesel engine or a gasoline engine, carburetor- or fuel-injector-fed) causes various items of control apparatus to achieve optimum spark or fuel-injection timing, fuel flow, and fuel-air ratio for the immediate circumstances. The microcomputer for a **Variable-Displacement Engine** also takes cylinders out of operation when conditions permit. It inactivates a cylinder by shifting the positions of valve-gear components to inactivate its intake and exhaust valves. By temporarily cutting a (say) eight-cylinder engine back to six or even four cylinders, it cuts the rate of fuel consumption.

**Spark Knock,** sometimes called **Ping,** a sound reminiscent of castenets, occurs on an up-grade or on acceleration. Ping is more pronounced the more the timing is advanced—that is, the earlier the spark occurs as the piston approaches the top of its travel. Ping can be eliminated entirely by retarding the spark sufficiently (i.e., making it occur later); but excessive retardation of the spark causes the engine to be sluggish, to run inefficiently, and to overheat. Timing specifications therefore represent a compromise between the two extremes, and when the timing is precisely right and the engine is receiving fuel of the proper grade (make a point of knowing this), a pinging sound will be faintly audible on rapid acceleration or under other conditions of high engine load, but not audible at all on level ground, or at steady speed up modest grades, or on modest acceleration.

Spark knock, or ping, is the result of explosive expansion of the burning fuel in a cylinder at a rate substantially greater than the descending piston can accommodate. It can be likened to a hammer blow inside the cylinder, striking cylinder head, cylinder wall, piston, connecting rod, and crankshaft; and just as a hammer blow causes a metallic object to ring or clang so does the shock wave produced by the fuel charge that is exploding too rapidly. If the ping could be avoided entirely it would be desirable, since the sound is evidence of abnormally high mechanical stress on the bearings inside the engine; but the faint ping of an engine that is properly tuned does not connote severe abuse, and the engine can take it without damage. You should be alert to ping when you drive, of course, and avoid pushing the engine with the accelerator to the point where the castenets are loud.

**High-Test Gasoline** causes less ping than "regular" grade of gasoline. Either because of its composition or because of anti-knock additives—the effect can be achieved either way—it burns a little less explosively than regular gasoline, and yet is able to deliver just as much power over the whole combustion stroke. Some automobile engines require high-test gasoline for best performance because they are designed to generate particularly high pressures in the cylinders on the compression stroke. (The higher the compression, the more power the fuel mixture generates on combustion. In most cases, high-compression engines will operate satisfactorily on regular gasoline if the spark is retarded slightly.) High-test gasoline does not yield any more miles-per-gallon. It should be used only if regular gasoline causes excessive spark knock in your engine. It may be worthwhile to depart from this rule to the extent of buying an occasional tank of high-test gasoline to combat "dieseling," or "after-run"—terms used to describe the irritating habit of some engines to continue to run, in a snorting manner, after the ignition has been turned off. Dieseling is usually caused by a combination of factors. The most prominent cause in most cases is too high an idling speed, but a second cause seems to be carbon deposits in the cylinders: the carbon continues to glow at red heat, and the red-hot carbon ignites the fuel mixture, without the need of the usual ignition spark. High-test gasoline burns somewhat more "cleanly" than low-test gasoline, and seems to burn away excessive carbon deposits. ((Dieseling can sometimes be prevented in a car with automatic transmission by keeping it in "drive" until after the engine stops; in a manual transmission car it is a simple matter to leave it in gear while shutting down, and let up on the clutch pedal if necessary to stop the engine.)

**Tune-up** is a term that is widely used, primarily in connection with the ignition systems of gasoline engines, but unfortunately it means different things to different people. The cost of a tune-up therefore varies widely, not only because garages have different labor rates, but also because they include different lists of inspections and repairs in what they call "a time-up." If yours is a non-electronic (i.e., a breaker-point) ignition system, the minimum tune-up includes inspecting and re-gapping or (usually) replacing the spark plugs, replacing distributor points, rotor, and condenser, and checking the timing and adjusting it if necessary. More conscientious mechanics inspect the manifold heat valve, the 12-volt wiring to the coil, and the high-voltage spark plug leads, wipe off and examine the coil body and distributor cap, check spark advance/retard devices on the distributor, and adjust hot and cold idling speeds. Still more conscientious mechanics may clean the battery posts, clean or replace the PCV valve, check fuel-pump output pressure, inspect the air filter, inspect all belts and hoses, and finally road test the car.

Electronic-ignition systems do not require breaker-point service, but they do require the other services listed above to the same extent that breaker-point systems do. The electronic component of the ignition system does not normally require routine "checking-out," but if engine operation is unsteady or otherwise unsatisfactory, the symptoms may point to the ignition system and require inspection and testing of the electronic unit. Microprocessors that control either gasoline or diesel engines often have built-in malfunction indicators. The checking-out procedure is unique to each system.

The term "tune-up" does not appear at all in the maintenance schedules of this book because it is such an ambiguous term. If your mechanic uses the term, you should find out what he includes in his routine tune-up service, so you will know what will—and more important—what will **not** be done.

## THE DRIVE TRAIN

The drive train transmits to the wheels the force generated by the engine, and thus causes the car to move. The drive train consists of a *clutch*, a *transmission*, a *drive shaft* and *universal joints*, a *differential*, *axles*, and *driving wheels*. (In a car with automatic transmission the clutch is not a separate component; it is incorporated into the transmission. In front-wheel-drive cars, the transmission and differential are combined in a *transaxle* unit.)

Automobiles that have **rear-wheel drive** with the engine located at the front are still the most popular. The next sketch shows the arrangement of components in such a car. Today, there are many front-wheel drive cars with the engine in front, and a few

with the engine mounted in the rear. Transmission repair is much
more costly for front-wheel drive vehicles. Most rear-engine cars
and front-wheel drive cars have **transverse engines**—that is, the
engine is not oriented fore-and-aft, as in the sketches in this book,
but crosswise. Wherever the engine may be located, however,
or in whatever direction it is pointed, the drive systems have the
components described here.

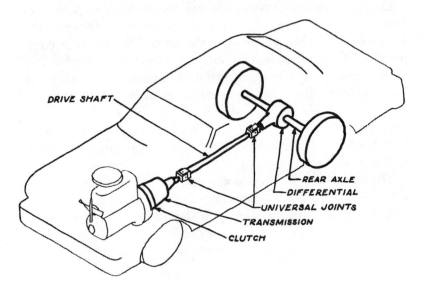

DRIVE SHAFT

REAR AXLE
DIFFERENTIAL
UNIVERSAL JOINTS
TRANSMISSION
CLUTCH

*Drive Train*

The **Transmission.** In order to understand why an internal-
combustion engine needs a transmission, it may be helpful first
to consider another kind of power. If we were to substitute an
electric motor of appropriate design for the combustion engine
in a car, we would not need a transmission at all. The drive shaft
would extend all the way forward to the motor, and would be
connected directly to it. To start a car from a standstill, we would
simply feed electric current from a battery to the motor, using

the kind of control knob that is on an electric stove; the car would then move forward. To accelerate faster, we would turn the knob to a higher setting; and when we got up to the speed we wanted, we would cut back on the setting a bit and the motor would hold the speed. There would be no need to start the motor first, as we must do with a combustion engine, and then shift into "drive," or, if we have a manual rather than an automatic transmission, shift into low, then second, then third, and perhaps into fourth gear, manipulating the clutch pedal and the accelerator pedal between shifts. Nor would we have to shift down to climb a hill or to accelerate faster, or let the motor idle when we stop at a traffic light. Our single concern would be that knob: turn it higher for more power, turn it down for less, turn it all the way off for a dead stop.

The major point of the electric motor in this connection is that it is capable of starting up under full load from zero speed, and it is capable of providing any amount of force, from none at all up to its maximum capacity, at any speed from zero to the speed at which it will destroy itself.

The combustion engine differs from the electric motor in its capabilities in several important respects, and it is the deficiencies of the combustion engine compared with the electric motor that make it necessary to provide a transmission in the automobile drive train.

*First:* an internal-combustion engine cannot be started under load. We must start the engine first, before connecting it to its load. Once started, it is ready to do its work of moving the car.

*Next:* a combustion engine turning at low speeds can provide only a weak force. It is not able to provide its maximum force until it gets up to relatively high speed. But great force is needed to accelerate an automobile from zero speed, rapidly enough to be practical. (You know how much harder it is to get a car in motion when pushing it, than to keep it going once you have it rolling.) Such levels of force can be achieved by a combustion engine only by "gearing down"—a term we will explain later.

*Next:* an internal-combustion engine should not be run at unnecessarily high speeds. Unlike an electric motor, it suffers excessive wear at very high speed; therefore, once an automobile
reaches cruising speed, and requires much less force than it required to be accelerated to that speed, the engine would be allowed
to drop back to the minimum speed at which it can do its job
of keeping the car going.

*Finally:* a combustion engine runs in one direction only, but
it is essential that the automobile be able to move backward as
well as forward. An electric motor can be made to run in reverse
simply by reversing the current supplied to it. In an automobile,
reverse motion can be achieved only by means of appropriate
arrangement of gears in the transmission.

The combination of **Clutch** and **Transmission** accommodates
the characteristics and needs of the gasoline engine.

The first need of the engine is to be permitted to start up and
run without moving the car, and then to take on the load of moving the car from a standstill without itself having to stop. The
clutch is the basic element that makes this possible.

The principle of the **Clutch** is illustrated in the next sketch.
A flat disc, or plate, is attached to the end of a shaft. A second
shaft is located end-on to the first, and the second shaft is fitted
with a disc that is movable longitudinally on the shaft. If the first
shaft and plate (the "driving shaft" and "driving plate,") are
rotating and the second plate is pushed up against the first, to
make face-to-face contact, then the second plate (the "driven
plate") and the shaft attached to it will also rotate. The second
plate will not begin instantaneously to rotate at the same speed
as the driving plate, of course; the two plate surfaces will slip
relative to one another at first, but the second plate will gradually
and smoothly come up to the speed of the driving plate. In an
automobile, the driving plate is almost always the rear face of
the engine flywheel, and the driving shaft is the crankshaft of
the engine. The driven shaft is connected with the driving wheels

of the car—indirectly, as will be described later, through the transmission, drive shaft, and differential.

Thus does the clutch mechanism make it possible for the engine to run while the car stands still (clutch disengaged), and to gradually increase the speed of the car from zero to a finite speed without stalling the engine (clutch plates slipping), and finally to drive the car forward (or backward) at a speed corresponding to the speed of crankshaft and flywheel (clutch engaged).

Note that each time the clutch plate is engaged or disengaged, some wear in the clutch plate occurs. Slippage between clutch surfaces is the essence of the clutch, and slippage causes wear. Note also that if you let your foot rest on the clutch pedal— known as "riding the clutch"—the weight of your foot will partially disengage the clutch, and thus cause slippage, and *cause the clutch plate to wear out prematurely. Don't ride the clutch!*

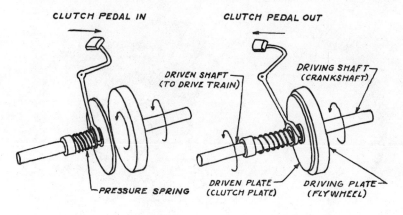

*Principle of the Clutch*

The second need of the gasoline engine is to operate within a comparatively narrow range of speeds—a much narrower range than we want our cars to operate. This need is met by selecting appropriate combinations of gears in a transmission unit.

A **Gear** is a wheel with teeth on its perimeter. If one gear is brought into peripheral contact with a second gear and if the teeth of the two mesh properly, then if one gear is rotated the other gear will rotate also. The next illustration shows a system of three gears that mesh together. Gear B is twice as large as Gear A and has twice as many teeth; and Gear C is two-thirds as large as Gear A and has two-thirds as many teeth. In this specific example, let us assume that Gear A drives Shaft B and Shaft C by way of the system of gears. When Shaft A, and with it Gear A, make one revolution, Gear B, and with it Shaft B, will make only one-half a revolution, since Gear B has twice as many teeth as Gear A. Similarly, when Shaft A makes one revolution Gear C, and with it Shaft C, will make one and one-half revolutions, since Gear A has half again as many teeth as Gear C.

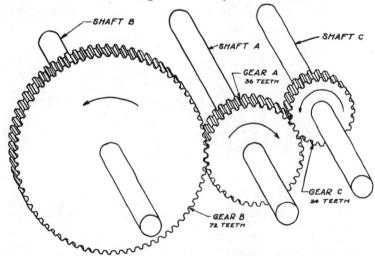

*Gearing up and gearing down*

The same relationships hold in the matter of *speed* of rotation: if Shaft A rotated at 100 revolutions per minute (RPM), then Shaft B would rotate at 50 RPM and Shaft C at 150 RPM. Shaft A would be said to be "geared down" to Shaft B, and "geared up" to Shaft C.

Another consequence of gearing up or gearing down is to alter the turning *force* of the shaft that is doing the driving—in this case the shaft that is connected to the engine. In the sketch, Gear B has twice as many teeth as Gear A: hence A must make two revolutions to cause B to revolve once, but the turning force imparted to Shaft B is twice that of Shaft A. The opposite is true in the case of Shaft C: Gear C is two-thirds as large as Gear A; hence Shaft C rotates half-again as fast as Shaft A, but turns with only two-thirds the force of A.

The principles just illustrated are employed in all automobile transmissions, automatic and manual, to enable the engine to operate within the speed range it can accommodate, and to multiply the turning force it is capable of providing.

The transmission matches engine speed to wheel speed. With rare exceptions this means *gearing down* the engine speed while the car is starting up. By the time you have shifted through second and third to high, the engine is no longer geared down: the drive shaft turns at the same speed as the engine.

Some circumstances will make an **overdrive** gear worthwhile. At cruising speed in flat country, for example, the engine can supply all the power that the wheels need by operating at *lower* speed than the drive shaft. Accordingly, some transmissions provide this overdrive gear, in addition to the conventional other gears, to enable the engine to work less at higher speeds.

In **Manual Transmission** cars, clutch operation must be coordinated with the shifting of gears, but the two actions are carried out independently by means of the clutch pedal and the gearshift lever, respectively. When the gearshift lever is in the "neutral" position, it interrupts the train of meshed gears inside the gearbox—so the car won't move if you let up on the clutch pedal. Before you move the lever to mesh the gears, however, you must push the pedal down to disengage the clutch. This permits the driven shaft to stop turning, whereupon you may engage the gears without damaging them.

When the **Automatic Transmission** is in "park" or "neutral," the engine is entirely disconnected from the drive train. At this setting, the engine may be started and operated at idling speed, ready for service, while the car is stationary. Shifted to "drive," the automatic transmission connects the engine to the drive train, in a loose way, while the engine is running at idling speed or not much above, and more firmly at higher speeds. When you speed up the engine, the car moves, first in low gear, then in second, and finally in high. In an automatic transmission, the clutch is incorporated in the gear-shifting and power-transmission mechanisms; it is not operated separately by the driver of the car.

**Transmission Fluid** is the medium through which this connecting and disconnecting is accomplished. This is a pool of fluid which rotates with the engine flywheel; a special kind of paddle-wheel immersed in the pool rotates with it; the paddle-wheel is attached to the drive train. The transmission fluid is also the medium which causes the gears to be shifted automatically in response to changes in speed and load.

The transmission component of a **Transaxle** may be either an automatic transmission or a manual transmission. If the latter, the transaxle unit also includes a pedal-operated clutch. The transaxle unit also incorporates the *differential*, which is a separate unit on front-engine rear-wheel-drive cars. The function of the differential is described in a later paragraph.

Front-wheel drive automobiles present a few unique problems. Besides the fact that front brakes tend to wear twice as fast and transmission repair costs are higher, there are two **constant velocity joints**, also called "CV" joints, per drive shaft. They must be monitored and maintained regularly. Check your owner's manual for details.

In the conventional drive-train arrangement shown in the sketch on page 108, the ultimate contribution of the power plant of the automobile is to cause an **output shaft** that protrudes from the rear of the transmission to rotate in the direction and at the speed you want the wheels to turn. The remainder of the drive train transmits this rotational force to the rear wheels.

A first requirement for successfully harnessing the output shaft to the rear wheels is physical flexibility. The wheels must be free to move up and down relative to the body of the car; but the engine and transmission are for all practical purposes bolted rigidly to the body. **Universal Joints** provide the flexibility in the drive train to accommodate the forward and rear elements of the system. Their location is shown in the sketch on page 108. A universal joint is essentially two hinges fastened to each other at right angles. Shafts attached to the two ends of the universal-joint assembly can be quite far out of alignment with each other and still turn freely without straining either the shafts or the coupling.

The **Drive Shaft** is a slender but sturdy hollow cylinder that runs underneath the car from about the midpoint to the rear. (The "hump" in the front passenger compartment of a rear-wheel-drive car is there to accommodate the transmission; the hump in the rear compartment accommodates the drive shaft.) The drive shaft, usually with a universal joint at each end, connects the transmission to the differential.

The **Differential** is an assembly of gears that enables two wheels that are driven by the same transmission output shaft to rotate at different speeds and still share equally the work of pushing the car forward. In a front-engine rear-wheel-drive car the differential unit is enclosed in a bulbous housing that is located about halfway between the rear wheels. What mechanics often refer to as "the rear end" of a rear-wheel-drive car is the assembly of differential and the **rear axles**—the transverse heavy housing onto which the rear brakes and rear wheels are attached, which encloses the differential gears and the rear axles.

In front-wheel-drive ("FWD") cars and also rear-engine, rear-wheel-drive cars, the differential system is incorporated in the transaxle unit, the output shafts protrude from the unit transversely instead of fore-and-aft, and there are two transverse drive shafts, one to each drive wheel, equipped with universal joints at each end. Many transaxle units are equipped with **dust boots** to protect universal joints from dirt and mud. These protective covers *are comparatively fragile, and they must be inspected carefully each time the car goes to the garage for service, at intervals not greater than 5,000 miles.* If a dust boot is in questionable condition, it must be replaced; failure of the seal could result in expensive damage within the transaxle assembly.

**Drive Train Maintenance** involves lubrication, lubricant changes, adjustments, and occasional component replacements, as follows:

Clutch-pedal adjustment should be checked every 15,000 miles. A maladjusted clutch will slip and will therefore wear at an accelerated rate—as though you "rode the clutch"—i.e., rested your foot on the pedal (which you should never do!). (Some cars have **self-adjusting clutches,** and so clutch adjustment can be dropped from the maintenance schedule for these cars.) Some cars have a **hydraulic clutch linkage** which should be checked at the regular 5,000-mile service intervals.

The clutch assembly will ultimately have to be overhauled. If you use your car mostly for short trips that require a lot of stopping and starting, or if your driving is mostly in traffic, your clutch will get a lot of wear and may have to be overhauled within 30,000 miles. If you drive mostly on highways where you use the clutch very little, it may last two or three times as long.("Hot-rodding," or otherwise demonstrating the superior getaway capabilities of your car, can reduce the life-expectancy of the clutch dramatically. "Riding the clutch" will also bring you in for a clutch overhaul in comparatively short order.)

Manual transmissions should be checked for oil level every 5,000 miles and oil added if needed. Even though the owner's manual of your car may say that "no service is needed" (a remarkable recommendation regarding any system of moving parts!), the transmission oil should be changed after 100,000 miles. If your owner's manual specifies shorter oil-change intervals, as many (particularly for front-drive cars) do, the recommendation should be followed.

Automatic-transmission fluid level should be checked and replenished if necessary at 5,000-mile intervals—or more frequently, if you become aware of oil spots (especially reddish oil) on the garage floor or parking-place pavement. Transmission fluid should be replaced and internal filters cleaned or replaced, and any appropriate internal adjustments should be made, every

25,000 miles. (Again, some owner's manuals, particularly for older cars, tell you that "no service is needed"—which, again, should be regarded as bad advice.) *Abnormal behavior* of automatic transmissions is usually caused by too little fluid in the system; and operating the transmission with inadequate fluid may damage the transmission. Therefore, if you notice *any* odd behavior of the car on moving either backward or forward, you should have the transmission-fluid level checked immediately.

If the universal joints can be lubricated (usually they can't in modern cars), they should be, at 5,000-mile intervals. (This operation is usually included in a chassis-lubrication job, but you should inquire specifically of your mechanic.) The life-expectancy of universal joints is of the order of 75,000 miles. Impending failure usually gives signals: vibration or noise or both.

In front-engine rear-drive cars, differential oil level should be inspected and oil added if needed at 5,000-mile intervals, and replaced at 100,000-mile intervals (again, whether or not the owner's manual prescribes it.) The rear axles are automatically lubricated by the oil in the differential.

## THE BRAKE SYSTEM

The brake system is the combination of pedals, pistons, cylinders, cables, levers, brake shoes or pads, and drums or discs which slow down and stop the car.

Braking action is achieved by pressing a pad or "shoe" against a rotating metal surface. A bicycle hand-brake illustrates the principle: you squeeze a lever against the handlebar, and a connecting cable causes two rubber pads to squeeze the rim of one of the wheels. Similarly, in an automobile with *disc brakes*, you push down on the brake pedal and two brake pads squeeze a rotating steel disc attached to each wheel. If the car has *drum brakes*, the rotating metal surfaces are not discs but shallow steel cylindrical cups that rotate with the wheels. In this case, the friction surfaces are called brake "shoes," and when you push down on the brake pedal these shoes are pushed outward against the inner surfaces of the drums. Brake shoe action in drum brakes is illustrated and a complete brake system is illustrated in the sketch on the next page.

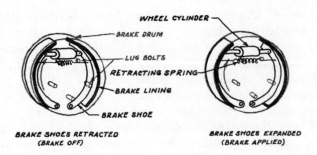

*Drum Brake Assembly*

The **Parking Brake** on your car operates in essentially the same way as the bicycle brake. When you pull the brake lever or push on the parking-brake pedal, cables cause the shoes or pads at the rear wheels (only) to be pressed against the drums or discs. This is also called the **Emergency Brake**, which serves to remind us that it can be used if the hydraulic system fails. It is not nearly as effective as the service brake, but it is better than no brake at all.

The **Service Brakes,** which are the brakes you use in normal operation of the car, have a different kind of linkage between the pedal and the wheels. The force you apply to the pedal is transmitted to the pads or shoes by means of a hydraulic system.

The **Hydraulic System** consists of a **Master Cylinder,** a **Wheel Cylinder** at each wheel, and **Brake Lines** and **Brake Hoses** that connect the cylinders. (Brake *lines* are not the same as brake *linings;* page 120.) Cylinders and hoses are completely filled with **Brake Fluid,** a special oil. All of these components except wheel cylinders appear in the next sketch; a wheel cylinder is shown above. (In disc-brake systems, the wheel cylinder is not a separate entity but instead is a component of a "caliper" assembly that includes the brake pads and the mechanism for squeezing the opposite faces of the disc between them.)

When you push on the brake pedal, a piston moves in the master cylinder and puts pressure on the brake fluid in the system, which in turn transmits the pressure to the wheel cylinders and the pistons in them. The increased pressure forces these pistons outward and causes them to exert force on the brake shoes or pads, pushing them against the drums or discs. (Hydraulic systems are described in some detail on page 162.) When you let up on the brake pedal, springs pull the shoes or pads away from the rotating surfaces.

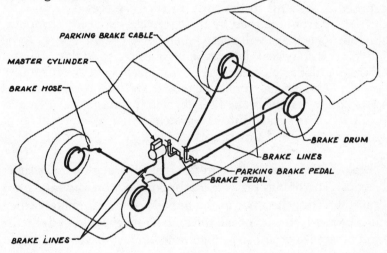

PARKING BRAKE CABLE

MASTER CYLINDER

BRAKE HOSE

BRAKE DRUM

BRAKE LINES

PARKING BRAKE PEDAL

BRAKE PEDAL

BRAKE LINES

*Brake System*

Beginning in 1967, and earlier in some makes, cars have *dual hydraulic systems* to operate the brakes. One hydraulic system operates the front brakes (or, in some cars, the left-front and the right-rear brakes), and a second system operates the brakes on the other two wheels. The brake pedal operates the pistons in the master cylinders of both systems, but the systems are hydraulically independent of each other. A dual system is much safer than a single system: a leak or piston failure will at worst deprive you of braking action on only two wheels, not all four. Braking action will be much reduced, but reduced braking action is better than no braking action at all. Many cars have **brake**

**warning lights** on the instrument panel that tell you if the pressures in the two hydraulic systems are not equal. Lacking such help, your warning that something is wrong will be the unusual feel of the brake pedal, its greater travel before braking action occurs, and of course the reduced braking effect.

**Brake Lines** and **Brake Hoses** should be inspected for leaks and physical damage at 5,000-mile intervals, when the car is up on the rack for changing oil. These lines and hoses are necessarily exposed to hazards in the form of rocks, pieces of scrap-iron thrown up from the road by the tires, and corrosion from outside. Gross leakage will cause an entire hydraulic system to be inoperative. Physical damage sometimes causes sudden failure. Corrosion damage usually gives you warning in the form of a "spongy" brake pedal: hydraulic fluid leaks out through corroded spots, and when the brake-fluid level in the master cylinder gets too low, air is sucked into the system. Air is compressible (liquids are not), and this causes the spongy feel in the pedal.

**Brake Linings** are the friction-resistant coverings on brake shoes or pads. The linings provide the braking action and take most (but not all) of the wear in the brake system. Ultimately, they must be replaced with new linings; the frequency depends on the kind of service your car is in and the kind of driver you are. A hot-rodder screeching his way through city traffic wears out linings every ten thousand miles or so. At the other extreme is the sensible driver whose car is used primarily on rural highways, and little if any in city traffic. In one case we know, a car that is used mostly for long-distance, high-speed traveling and almost not at all for stop-and-go city driving, the brakes needed no attention other than periodic inspection in their first 90,000 miles.

As brake linings are worn away, the brake shoe must travel further in order to make contact with the steel drum or disc. In the case of disc brakes, the greater travel is a negligible matter; but with drum brakes, the effect is magnified and unless something is done about it, the amount of pedal travel required to apply the brakes would increase quite markedly. Drum-brake mechanisms are therefore adjustable to compensate for wear of the brake linings, and most are equipped with a self-adjusting mechanism that operates when the car moves in reverse and the brakes are applied.

Oil, grease, or brake fluid on a brake lining has the paradoxical effect of increasing the friction between the lining and the drum or disc, and making the brake "grab." Water has the opposite effect: it lubricates the lining, and reduces friction between lining and metal surface. In either case, if only one wheel is affected, its braking action will be markedly different from its opposite number and the car will swerve when you apply the brakes. The effect is more pronounced in front brakes than in rear brakes, but it is not trivial in either case, especially on slippery pavements. If all four brakes are water-soaked, braking action is very poor and the situation may be dangerous if it takes you by surprise.

Wet brake linings can be dried by applying the brakes a few times, or even by holding the brake pedal down lightly while moving the car ahead at low speed; the heat thus generated will evaporate the water and dry out the linings.

Brake linings that have been fouled with grease from a wheel bearing (usually thanks to a leaky grease seal, called a "grease retainer") or with brake fluid (thanks to a leaky wheel cylinder) can sometimes be simply cleaned off and restored to service if attended to promptly enough. Usually, however, it is necesssary to replace the brake linings, and this means replacing linings not only on the affected wheel but also the corresponding one on the other side, since it is essential that braking action be identical on right and left wheels.

A **Power Brake** system is the standard hydraulic system with the addition of a "vacuum booster" interposed between the brake pedal and the master cylinder. When you push on the brake pedal in this system you activate a valve that causes vacuum to be pulled on one side of a large diaphragm; the vacuum causes magnified force to be exerted on the piston in the master cylinder.

If for some reason the source of vacuum fails, then the force you exert on the pedal will be transmitted directly to the piston in the master cylinder, but it will not be amplified by the "vacuum assist." Without this vacuum assist, power brakes are considerably less effective even than ordinary brakes; the system is designed to use the vacuum assist, and when that is not present the brake pedal gives less leverage, and hence much more force must be applied to achieve braking action.

The engine supplies the vacuum for power brakes. If the engine stops, the vacuum will deteriorate rapidly. If your power brake system seems at all erratic or uncertain when the engine is running normally, have your mechanic investigate it immediately. To be unexpectedly deprived of power in your power brakes can be dangerous.

**The Brake System
is the Most Important System of all:
Pay Attention to These Symptoms.**

a.  If the brake pedal can be pushed to the floor . . . This means that the hydraulic system has failed completely and that your service brakes are not working. Drive carefully to a garage, using your parking (emergency!) brake.

b.  If the brake warning light goes on . . . This means that the hydraulic system that serves two of the wheels has failed, and that only the brakes on the other two wheels are working. Drive cautiously to a garage.

c.  If you can push the brake pedal down further than normal . . . This probably means that one of the hydraulic systems has failed, as described above in b.

d.  If pedal travel has increased gradually and is now substantially greater than you consider "normal" . . . The brakes probably need adjusting; your brake system may not have a self-adjusting mechanism, or, if it does, it may not be functioning.

e.  If the brake pedal feels "spongy" . . . This means that you have lost brake fluid from the system, and air has been sucked in to replace it. Serious further trouble may develop right away. Drive cautiously to a garage immediately.

f. If the brakes grab or the car pulls to one side when you apply the brakes . . . The linings may be wet from deep puddles of water on the pavement, or they may be wet from oil or grease or brake fluid which has leaked out at one or more wheels. Drive with particular care, especially on slippery pavements, until you can get to a garage.

g. If the brakes drag—i.e., if the car does not coast freely, but behaves as though the brakes are being applied lightly when they are not . . . This means that an automatic-adjustment mechanism in one or more wheel assemblies is not functioning properly and the brakes do not release completely. Have the brakes inspected as soon as you can.

h. If the brakes squeal when you apply them, it may mean that the linings need replacing. Some linings have wire springs embedded in them; these become exposed when the lining wears down, and make a squealing sound when they rub against the steel disc or drum. Brake squeal may also be caused by other things: the hardness and nature of the lining, or dirt.

Routine brake system maintenance should include:

1. Inspect the brake-fluid levels on the occasion of each oil change. This is normally done routinely, but mention it specifically. Also, request when the car is on the rack for changing the oil, that brake lines and hoses be inspected for leaks and damage.

2. Have the service brakes adjusted if pedal travel, having increased gradually, becomes about twice what you consider to be normal pedal travel.

3. Have brake linings inspected for wear after the first 20,000 miles of city driving or 30,000 miles of country or turnpike driving, and at intervals of 10,000 miles thereafter, unless you and your mechanic decide on some other schedule.

4. When brake linings need replacing on a pair of wheels, have brake drums or discs reconditioned (called "turning") and brake hoses and wheel cylinders or caliper assemblies replaced, unless the component under consideration is unquestionably in excellent condition. If the wheel bearings are of the type that require periodic lubricating, have the bearings repacked if they are due for service within a few thousand miles.

5. Have the parking brake adjusted as needed, to correct excessive travel of parking-brake pedal or lever.

6. Replace all metal brake lines at intervals of 100,000 miles or 10 years, whichever comes first, and also replace any brake hoses that are more than five years (or 50,000 miles) old.

*Note that front-wheel drive vehicles experience a much more rapid deterioration of the front brakes, requiring the brakes to be checked more frequently.*

## THE SUSPENSION SYSTEM

The suspension system is the collection of levers, hinges, springs, pistons, and cylinders that hold up the frame, the engine, the transmission, and the body, away from the wheels, and cushion them and the passengers from the roughness of the road surface. When a wheel encounters a bump or a pot-hole, it moves—or at high speed it bounces—up and down. Ideally, the suspension system would entirely absorb this up-and-down movement, and the car and its occupants would glide smoothly through space. In practice, all of the many kinds of suspension systems that have been tried fall considerably short of this ideal.

Numerous suspension-system designs are in use today. In the following paragraphs we describe the oldest established front and rear suspension systems that are still in use, and thereafter describe the most important subsequent variations on those systems that are incorporated in other present-day systems.

The prototype **Rear Suspension** is simply a pair of *leaf springs* and a pair of *shock absorbers*, as shown in the next sketch. The

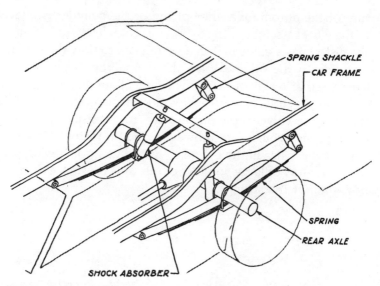

*Leaf-Spring Rear Suspension*

springs permit the wheels to move up and down relative to the frame and body. The spring leaves are "arched," and when the body is bounced up and down on the wheels, the leaves become straighter as the body goes down, and become more roundly arched as the body bounces upward. Note that the spring assembly is hinged to the frame at its forward end; the *spring shackle* accommodates the changes in horizontal length of the leaves as their curvature changes under the varying load.

A **Shock Absorber** at each wheel moderates the bounciness of the springs and helps keep the car steady and under control. The preceding sketch shows shock absorbers in place in a rear suspension system, and gives some idea of both their location and their appearance. The body of a shock absorber is a cylinder that is closed at both ends; inside is a piston, the rod of which protrudes through a leak-proof seal at the upper end of the cylinder. (Cylinder-and-piston assemblies are described more generally on page 160.) The piston rod is attached to the frame or a body struc-

ture of the automobile; the bottom of the cylinder is attached
to the wheel assembly. The cylinder is completely full of oil, and
the piston has a valve in it that permits oil to flow through from
one side to the other. When the piston rod is pushed down
slowly—that is, when the car is riding along on a smooth road
with only gentle up-and-down movement—oil flows readily
through the valve in the piston with little resistance. If the car
travels over a rough spot, however, and the piston is jerked one
way or the other in the cylinder, the valve in the piston resists
the rapid flow of large volumes of oil. This resistance damps the
bounding of the springs.

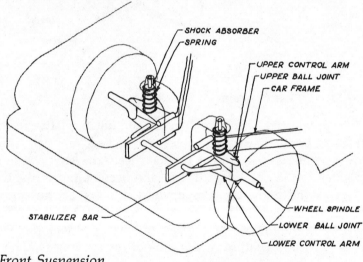

*Front Suspension*

The **Front Suspension** shown in the above sketch is the kind
that has been used for decades on rear-wheel-drive cars, and is
on the vast majority of such cars that are in service today. Again,
the wheels must be free to move up and down relative to the body,
but they must also be permitted to swivel from side to side to
steer the car. It is important to stability of steering to hold the
front wheels in a perpendicular stance as they bounce up and
down. It is for this reason that two *control arms* rather than only

one are associated with each front wheel. The control arms are hinged to the frame at their inner ends, and at their outer ends to the *wheel spindles* by means of *ball joints*.

**Ball Joints** are ball-and-socket joints similar in principle to human shoulder and hip joints. They permit the control arms to swing up and down freely, and also permit the wheel spindles (and the front wheels, which the spindles serve as axles) to swivel. Ball joints are intended to endure a great deal of wear, and are designed and built to be lubricated regularly to prolong their life. **Control Arm Bushings** are replaceable hinge elements at the inner ends of the control arms which, together with the *control arm bolts*, hinge the control arms to the frame. ("Bushing" is defined more generally on page 158.) The bushings are made of wear-resistant metal and are also, on many cars, designed and built to be lubricated regularly.

A **Stabilizer Bar,** sometimes called a **Sway Bar,** is included in the front suspension systems of most cars, and in the rear suspension systems of many. The sketch on page 126 shows a stabilizer bar in place. Its primary purpose is to combat the tendency of the wheel on the inside of a curve, to lift off of the road surface. In addition, it enhances the steadiness of the suspension system.

Variations on the above prototype systems and on individual components of those systems that are used in present-day cars include *coil-spring rear suspension*, the *MacPherson Strut*, *torsion springs*, and *air-adjustable shock absorbers*.

The **Coil-Spring Rear Suspension** uses coil springs rather than the leaf springs of the system shown in the sketch on page 125. The coil springs are mounted vertically (as in the sketch on page 126) between the axles and the frame. Something more is needed, however, since coil springs have essentially no lateral rigidity, and would permit the car body to sway from side to side intolerably. (This problem is not encountered with leaf springs, since they have high lateral rigidity.) To prevent swaying from side to side and fore and aft, a heavy longitudinal lever on each side of the car is hinged at its front end to the frame and at its rear end to the rear-axle housing—just as the front half of each leaf spring is mounted. These levers are called *trailing arms*, or, alternatively, *rear control arms*.

An alternative to the front suspension system shown in the sketch on page 126, and one that is used on many front-wheel-drive cars, is the **MacPherson Strut** system. This system uses the lower control arm and lower ball joint described previously, but not the upper control arm and ball joint. Instead, the wheel spindle is attached rigidly to the body of the shock absorber. The shock absorber serves as the bearing in which the wheel spindle can swivel. The front spring is usually coiled around the shock absorber, as in the sketch.

**Torsion Springs** are used on some cars, in the front suspension, or the rear suspension, or both. A steel rod or bar or beam resists twisting, and if it is caused to twist by an applied force, it will spring back when the force is withdrawn—just as a coil spring, for example, will return to its previous height when a load is removed from it. The stabilizer bar shown in the sketch on page 126 could serve as a torsion spring if it were firmly secured at its center to prevent the whole U-shaped member from rotating in its mountings. If this member rather than the coil springs carried the weight of the car body, it would twist under the load, and twist more when a wheel encountered a bump or pot-hole, and then bounce back, and so on. (The so-called *twist-beam axle* that is used on the rear suspensions of some front-wheel-drive cars is a version of the suspension bar portrayed in the sketch.) Some torsion springs consist of *longitudinal* bars that are parallel to the frame, mounted so that the ends cannot rotate in their mountings. The lower control arm is rigidly mounted to the center of the torsion bar, so that the bar absorbs the load and shock by twisting; hence it serves as a main front spring of the vehicle.

**Air-Adjustable Shock Absorbers** are similar to conventional shock absorbers, but have the feature of an additional internal reservoir that can be elongated by injecting compressed air. The air cushion takes some of the load from the springs, and so the body of the car rides higher; but the damping of spring-bounce, the primary function of a shock absorber, is still achieved in the conventional way, by the hydraulic system inside the shock absorber. Some cars are equipped with an **automatic leveling system:** a sensor turns on an under-hood air compressor when the car is riding too low, to inflate the shock absorbers, or lets air out of the shock absorbers when the car is riding too high.

**Wheels** and **Tires** are not, strictly speaking, parts of the suspension system, but the ills and ailments of wheels and tires strongly affect the performance of the suspension system, and ailments and maladjustments of the suspension system strongly affect the performance of tires.

*Tire wisdom* is hard to come by, thanks to both the advertising hype that plagues our society and the fondness for old-wives' tales that plagues all societies. However, there appears to be reasonably good agreement, among writers and mechanics we talk with, along these lines: (1) the car "handles" best if all four tires are of the same type: all bias-ply, or all belted-bias-ply, or all radial, or all belted-radial: (2) bias-ply and belted bias-ply can be mixed safely, but it is slightly preferable to have the front tires match each other and the rear tires match each other; (3) the same general rule and slight preference pertain to radial and belted-radial tires; (4) radial or belted-radial tires on the front and bias-ply or belted-bias-ply tires on the rear make the car hard to steer (some say dangerously so); but radials (either type) on the rear and bias-ply (either type) on the front is an acceptable combination. The manufacturer of your car recommends the size. Unless the owner's manual says otherwise, a set of four radial tires is usually worthwhile. Select a 4-ply rated radial with a good flow-through tread pattern for a comfortable ride.

**Wheel Balancing.** Each wheel-and-tire combination should be balanced so that it will not wobble, bounce or vibrate when it turns at high speed. Few tires and wheels are uniform in weight all the way around. Balancing involves attaching weights to the rim of a wheel to compensate for heaviness on the opposite side. Static balancing is done with the wheel off the car: the weights are added to make the wheel lie level on a pointed spindle. Dynamic balancing is done by spinning the wheel and tire mounted on the car, or on a machine especially designed for this purpose. Although static balancing usually gives acceptable results, dynamic balancing is preferable since it simulates high-speed service, and it is at high speeds that vibration is most troublesome. Occasionally an unbalanced tire or wheel wobbles from side to side at high speed. Static testing cannot detect this kind of flaw.

**Tire Inflation.** It is important to keep the air pressure in the tires at least as high and preferably two or three pounds higher than the pressure specified in the owner's manual of your car. If tire pressure is too high, traction on the road surface will not be as good as it should be. If the pressure is too low, which is more likely, tire life will suffer, and the tires will be much more likely to blow out at highway speeds. The reason for this is that "soft" tires flex more than tires should, and this generates excessive heat, sometimes even to the point of almost melting the rubber. Rubber has much lower strength at high temperatures, and so the tire simply disintegrates.

Tire-inflation specifications always refer to pressure when the tires are cold. When the tire heats up, the pressure increases, often as much as five or six pounds per square inch. Let it. The tire is designed to take this increase in pressure—and in fact the higher pressure reduces the amount of flexing. *Never* let air out of a tire to bring its pressure down to "specifications" when the tire is hot.

**Tire Rotation** at 10,000-mile intervals compensates for differences in the patterns of tire wear that are unavoidable because of the geometry of the suspension system and, to a lesser extent, of crowned-surface roadways. "Cross-switching" accommodates both front-vs.-rear differences and high-side/low-side differences (left-rear tire moved to right-front wheel, and right-rear to left-front), and bias-ply tires should be rotated in this pattern. Radial tires are sensitive to direction of rotation, however, and therefore they should not be switched from one side to the other, but only front to rear and rear to front on the same side.

**Suspension-System Maintenance:**

1. Ball joints require periodic lubrication. New ones normally have rubber seals to keep water and dirt out and lubricant in. We recommend that they nevertheless be lubricated every 5,000 miles or at whatever interval your owner's manual recommends for oil changes.

2. Control arm bushings should be lubricated on the same schedule as ball joints—if they can be lubricated at all.

3. The rear-suspension assembly normally "requires no servicing"—meaning that no provision has been made for lubricating any of the joints.

4. Tires should be rotated every 10,000 miles, so that tires will wear as evenly as possible and yield maximum mileage: "fore-and-aft" switching in the case of radial tires, and "cross-switching" in the case of bias-ply tires.

5. The under-side of the car should be checked for rust damage when the odometer reaches 25,000 miles, and at 10,000-mile intervals thereafter. This check should include the frame (if your car has a frame), all fastenings of the suspension and the steering-gear to the frame, and all suspension-system and steering-system joints. This is particularly important if your car is of so-called *monocoque, unitized body,* or *unibody* construction—i.e., if it doesn't have an independent frame. Neglect of the under side can result in unnecessarily expensive damage, *or even separation of suspension-system or steering-system components from the body of the car!*

6. The **front-end alignment** should be checked every 15,000 miles and corrected if necessary. Misalignment causes abnormal wear of the front tires, and it may cause the car to "lead" to one side or the other unless you restrain it with the steering wheel, or to shimmy, or to squeal excessively on turns. The front end goes out of alignment because of severe mechanical shocks (potholes, curbs, parking-lot spacing barriers, etc.); but even if spared all these hazards (which it seldom is), the front-end will ultimately become misaligned as a result of natural wear in the joints of the suspension and steering systems. Re-aligning involves making any needed adjustments in front-wheel camber (inward or outward lean), caster (forward or rearward lean of the wheel spindles), and toe-in (pigeon-toedness, to compensate for the tendency of the tires to splay out when the car is in motion).

7. **Wheel bearings** must be lubricated periodically, if they can be lubricated, and adjusted if they are adjustable. Not included in this generalization are the rear-wheel bearings of most rear-drive cars, because the wheel bearings receive lubricant automatically from the differential unit. Front-wheel bearings and the rear-wheel bearings of front-drive cars should be cleaned, to remove old grease, and lubricated (mechanics call it "packing" the wheel bearings) at 25,000-mile intervals. New **grease retainers** should be installed each time wheel bearings are lubricated. Grease retainers are replaceable seals which prevent grease from the wheel bearings from seeping out and fouling the brake linings. Most mechanics routinely replace grease retainers whenever they re-pack wheel bearings, but it would do no harm to mention that you are aware of this practice and do not disapprove of it.

Your schedule of overhauling brakes may be close enough to 25,000 mile intervals so that you can do wheel-bearing lubrication and brake-overhauling on the same schedule. Even if this is not so, however, you should know whether your mechanic re-packed the wheel bearings when he overhauled the brakes, so that you will not have the job repeated earlier than it is needed. Front-wheel drive cars should have the front brakes serviced more often, however.

8. **Shock absorbers** have a life-expectancy of 20,000 to 50,000 miles, depending upon the condition of the roads and streets you travel on, and the speed of your traffic. Indications of worn shock absorbers are bounciness, some kinds of irregular tire wear, tire "tramp", front-wheel shimmy, wheel-hopping on hard acceleration or braking, and any general feeling of unsteadiness on moderately good pavement. Shock absorbers should preferably be replaced in sets of four; and at minimum, both at front or both at the rear should be replaced at the same time.

9. **Front-end overhaul** will ultimately be required to combat looseness in the front suspension. Excessive ball-joint wear is apparent to the mechanic when he is not longer able to restore wheel camber to specification value. (Some ball joints are now equipped with *wear indicators* which assist in diagnosis.) Control-arm bushings and bolts are replaceable, but not necessarily on the same schedule as ball joints. The links that connect the stabilizer or sway bar to the control arms or wheel spindles usually have replaceable ends. The entire front end should be inspected thoroughly whenever you become aware of unsteadiness up front. New front-end components can often make the car feel better and the driver more cheerful.

10. **Spring height** decreases very gradually, over a period of years: the springs "sag," and let the car body ride closer to the ground. Front-spring sag, if it becomes serious enough, can interfere with the alignment of the front end; but even before that, sagging springs can contribute appreciably to your dissatisfaction with your car. Leaf springs can be re-arched or replaced and coil springs and torsion springs can be replaced at moderate cost, to restore the new-car ride and feel. Alternatives to discuss with your mechanic are "helper" springs of several kinds and inflatable rubber bags that fit inside coil springs. These are used primarily to increase the load-carrying capacity of conventional car springs, but this does not preclude their use to combat sag.

## THE STEERING SYSTEM

The steering system is the assembly of shafts, gears, rods, levers, and swivels that translate your turning of the steering wheel into a change in the direction of the front wheels. The steering wheel rotates a shaft which turns gears in a steering box; beyond that is a series of arms, levers, rods, and joints that together cause the front wheels to swivel. The next sketch illustrates a typical steering system on a rear-wheel-drive car. In front-wheel-drive cars, the wheel spindles are replaced by power axles that drive the front wheels, and the steering mechanism must be designed to accommodate the drive-shaft-and-universal-joint assemblies to which the power axles are attached.

Most cars employ a **worm and segment** arrangement in the steering box. **Rack-and-pinion** steering is used in many sports cars. In both systems, a gear on the steering shaft drives a gear that transmits movement down the line, to make the pitman arm swing (worm-and-segment system), or to push directly on the relay rod (rack-and-pinion system).

Each of the numerous joints and gears in the steering assembly suffers a minute amount of wear each time you rotate or jiggle the steering wheel, and over a period of years appreciable looseness develops in the steering system. The change occurs so gradually that you may not even be aware of it, but in time the steering becomes much less steady and less responsive than it was originally. If you have it inspected regularly, it is not likely to become so loose as to be dangerous, but a loose steering mechanism makes a car feel old. Looseness and insteadiness in a steering system can be completely cured no matter how old the car or how far it has gone.

**Steering System Maintenance** requirements vary with the make and age of the car. In some cars, most or all of the joints are "lubricated for life" when they are manufactured. This means, in effect, that there is nothing you can do to prolong their lives. In other cars, some or all of the joints in the steering system are said by their owner's manuals to require lubrication only at intervals of 20,000 or even 36,000 miles. As far back as the early Seventies, however, manufacturers began to back away from such light-heartedness, and now the earlier wisdom of 5,000- or 6,000-mile intervals for lubricating suspension and steering systems tends to prevail. *We* believe it is foolish to gamble on long lubrication intervals. Front-end lubrications are not expensive, so you won't spend large sums of money if you lubricate frequently in an effort to forestall early replacement of parts.

The entire system should be checked critically for looseness at 25,000 miles and at 10,000-mile intervals thereafter. Looseness in the gear box can be corrected by making adjustments; looseness in the joints can be corrected only by replacing the joints. Replacement of a joint is not very expensive, and in view of the difference the condition of the steering system can make in your state of mind about the car, as well as in its ultimate safety, you should make it clear to your mechanic that you want him to replace any loose joint.

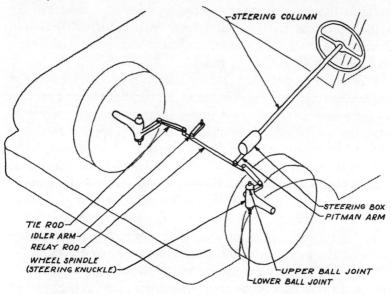

*Steering System*

**Power Steering** differs from the system shown in the sketch in that a **hydraulic booster** is incorporated into the system, and the steering wheel merely controls the booster. Power steering fluid under pressure does substantially all the work of operating the levers and rods that cause the front wheels to swivel. If for some reason the booster fails to function, the steering wheel can still control the front wheels, but a considerable effort is required of the driver.

The **Power Steering Pump** and the **Power Steering Fluid** work together to provide the power for the power steering system. The pump, located at the front of the engine on the left side, is driven by a belt which in turn is driven by the engine; hence it operates only when the engine is running. When the engine stops, the pump stops, and the whole power steering system immediately dies. The car can still be steered without the help of the power system, but the steering is much more difficult.

The life expectancy of power steering pumps varies widely, and cannot be given in terms of mileage. A pump is not likely to fail without warning for any reason other than failure of the belt that drives it; this belt (along with other belts) should therefore be checked for condition and tightness every 5,000 miles, and replaced every 25,000 miles.

Warning of approaching failure is usually given by leakage of the power steering fluid. This is an oily liquid, put into motion by the power steering pump, and it is the agent that really does the work of steering. It is important that the level of this fluid be kept up; therefore it is sensible to check it once a month, when you check the engine oil, the radiator, and the other crucial levels, and add fluid if it is needed. If you have to add more than about two ounces a month, you have a leak beginning, and you should have your mechanic look into it. Leaky steering-fluid hoses or hose connection are the most likely source of the trouble; worn seals on the pump or the steering box run a remote second.

If the fluid gets low enough so that the pump might be damaged, the pump will make a buzzing sound that can be heard when the engine is idling. The car may be driven five miles or so with the pump making this noise without damaging the system, but it is important to get to a filling station quickly and add fluid.

## LIGHTS AND ELECTRICAL EQUIPMENT

The lights and electrical equipment on an automobile operate on 12-volt current supplied by the battery. Wires, switches, and equipment in this kind of system can overheat, and make sparks, and even catch fire, but there is no danger in a car of being electrocuted.

Almost all electrical circuits in an automobile depend upon what is called "ground," that is, body, frame or engine to serve as a return path for the electric current. (See page 51 for a description of the term "ground.") Rusted joints anywhere along the ground path can cause lights to behave in mysterious ways. This is so commonplace that when any light or electrical accessory on your car acts in a manner you don't understand, the first thing to look for is a rusted ground connection.

**Fuses** play the same role in an automobile as they do in a house: they "blow" when there is prolonged overload on the electrical system that might start a fire or damage a component. Automobile fuses are slender glass tubes with metal ends, about an inch long or less. They are not screwed into fuse sockets, as in household systems, but are snapped into position between clips.

Most automobile circuits are protected by fuses, so if a windshield wiper or the heater blower or the radio won't operate, it may merely mean that a fuse needs to be replaced. Check the fuse first in the failure of any electrical system.

In some automobiles, virtually the entire electrical system is protected by a master fuse that is called a **Fusible Link**. Like the master fuse in a house, the fusible link almost never "blows," but when it does, nothing electrical in the car will operate. Your mechanic can tell you if your car is equipped with one of these master fuses (often the owner's manual doesn't mention it); if it does, you should always carry a spare.

**Circuit Breakers** are normally used instead of fuses in headlight-tail-light circuits. The reason for this is that circuit breakers interrupt the current only temporarily, and thus give you warning that something is wrong, without shutting off the lights completely and leaving you stranded. If your headlights fluctuate in intensity or go off, then back on, then off, it means the circuit breaker is responding to an overload somewhere in the circuit and is trying to tell you about it. You are not likely to do any further damage if you limp home in this condition, but you should have the problem investigated immediately because it may worsen rapidly.

**Headlight Adjustment** can be done by most filling stations; it is not an expensive job. Remember, though, that heavy loads in the rear of the car make the car ride low in back and this in turn causes the headlight beams to point higher than normal. Oncoming drivers may be angrily flashing their lights at you not because your headlights have suddenly gone out of adjustment, but because you have added a heavy load to the trunk or the rear passenger compartment.

**Headlight Covers**, the eyelids that cover the headlights of some cars pop up out of the way when the headlights are turned on, but are caused to pop up by vacuum provided by the engine. If your car is equipped with headlight covers, you should learn, from your owner's manual or from your mechanic, how to raise them by hand and keep them up out of the way, in case the vacuum mechanism should fail some dark night.

**Light Switches** in wide variety are used in the lighting system of an automobile. It is of course essential that the switches for the headlight, the stop light, the low beam-high beam and the turn indicator be replaced promptly if they go bad, since they are all necessary to the safe and lawful operation of the car. All the other switches can be replaced, too, generally speaking at modest cost; so there is no need to get along without passenger-compartment lights, trunk lights, glove-compartment lights, and other lights that make your car easier and pleasanter to drive.

The **Turn-Signal Switch** is located underneath the steering wheel. It is one of the few switches that is expensive to replace, since the steering wheel must be removed to get at it, and the switch assembly itself is more expensive than most. Failure of the turn-indicator switch most often takes the form of failure of the "canceling" mechanism—that is, the turning-off of the signals after you have made the turn. The mechanism depends on a piece of tough, resilient plastic; it will last for many years if it is not abused, and you can add immeasurably to its life expectancy if you will refrain from keeping your finger on the lever after you have switched it on. The turn-signal lever should not be restrained from returning to neutral, since this puts great strain on the mechanism. You can reduce the likelihood of your ever having to repair the turn-signal switch if you develop the habit of returning it to neutral manually.

The flasher unit that causes the turn-signal and emergency light to blink on and off is an inexpensive plug-in unit which on most cars is very easy to replace.

The **Windshield Wiper** and the **Windshield Washer** are often combined into a single unit in which the electric motor that drives the wiper blades also drives a water pump that squirts water through tubing and jets to the windshield. Other cars have separate washer pumps which are independent of the windshield wiper, but the control switches on the two units are normally inter-connected. (If the washer mechanism on a combined unit gives trouble, it is sometimes less expensive to install an independent washer pump than to overhaul the combined unit.) Washer pumps normally depend upon rubber or plastic check valves to effect their pumping action, and these require replacing occasionally, but the wiper and (usually) washer mechanisms themselves are long-lived. If the washer jets plug up, they can usually be cleaned with a fine wire or a pin of small diameter.

Windshield-washer systems require antifreeze in winter. Radiator antifreeze is not satisfactory for this service because it leaves gummy materials behind when it evaporates. Special antifreeze compounds are available for windshield washers.

Windshield Wiper Blades become smeary as they wear out, but a smeary blade is not necessarily worn—it may merely be fouled with oil and dirt. Automobiles travel in a cloud of oil mist that is sprayed in the air by all automobiles. The wiping edge of the windshield wiper blade picks up oil from the air and from the windshield, and the oil layer traps particles of dust and grit that prevent the blade from making good contact with the glass. Filling-station attendants seldom if ever clean the blades, however conscientious they may be about cleaning the windshield itself. Kitchen scouring powder is effective on wiper blades—but you may have to do this job yourself.

The **Heater,** the **Defroster,** and the **Air-Conditioner** are usually connected together in a single unit that uses a single electric blower to deliver either heated or cooled air through a system of ducts. Most present-day systems automatically turn on the heater or the air-conditioner, as appropriate, in response to the setting of the control thermostat. A vacuum system actuates the valves.

Two independent radiators are needed, one for heating and one for cooling. When you set the controls to "heat," hot water from the engine flows through a small radiator, known as the heater core. Air is blown over this hot surface, warmed, and then blown out into the passenger compartment. When you set the control to "defrost," you cause a damper valve in the duct system to divert the warmed air to narrow slits underneath the windshield. (Air-cooled engines do not use liquid coolant, so there is not hot liquid to supply a heater. Such a car is ordinarily equipped with a flameless gasoline-burning heater. It depends upon a glow-plug to start the combustion.)

When you set the controls to "cool," chilled refrigerant flows into the cooling radiator. Air is blown over the cold surface, cooled, and then blown out into the passenger compartment.

Air-conditioning requires a considerable amount of power, and for this reason affects the fuel consumption of the car quite substantially. The blower, of course, requires some power, but by far the greater power requirement is for operating the compressor that sucks refrigerant vapor from the refrigeration core and compresses it to convert it to a liquid. Thus, if you can use the blower alone for cooling on some occasions, you can save somewhat on your gas consumption.

The air-conditioning unit should be operated at the maximum cooling setting for a minimum of five minutes each month, in winter as well as in summer, to circulate the refrigerant and the oil that is mixed with it. This will lubricate the seals that hold refrigerant in the system, and help maintain their effectiveness. Also, you should have the air conditioner checked at 5,000-mile intervals for refrigerant level, to assure that you will have refrigeration when you want it.

Heater cores sometimes develop leaks and require repair or replacement, just as do main cooling-system radiators. A leaking heater core is one possible source of dampness of the front-compartment on the right-hand side; the other likely source is a leaky windshield gasket.

The **Power Seat** is moved back and forth and up and down by a heavy-duty electric motor and appropriate gears, levers, and screw threads underneath the seat. The motor and accompanying mechanism are ruggedly built and not likely to fail during the lifetime of the car. The control switch with which the driver controls the mechanism is also ruggedly built. If the unit fails to work, the fuse should be checked first, and then the switch.

If the action of the power seat should become sluggish, or its range of movement reduced, the mechanism should be cleaned and oiled. The seat mechanism is located where dust and dirt are at their thickest.

**Power Windows, Power Antennas, Convertible Tops** and similar mechanized apparatus are usually, like the power seat, provided with motors and drive mechanisms of rugged construction and long life expectancy. As in the case of the power seat, when you have trouble with these things, the fuse should be checked first and the control switch next, before you begin to suspect the mechanism itself.

All of the **gauges** (except the speedometer) and **warning lights** on the instrument panel are electrically activated. For example, the oil pressure warning light, described on page 59, turns on when an **oil-pressure switch** closes, which it does if the pressure in the engine lubrication system is lower than a pre-set minimum safe level. Similarly, if the pressure in one of the two brake (hydraulic) systems is higher than the pressure in the other, the pressure imbalance closes a similar switch and this turns on the brake warning light, described on page 119. The **coolant-temperature switch** responds to temperature: when it is higher than a pre-set value, the switch closes and the "hot" light (page 90) goes on. The **charging light** (page 94) goes on if the battery voltage is different from the alternator output voltage, which it will be if the alternator is not charging.

Other **sending units** are not simply "on-off" switches but are *rheostats* (like the controls on an electric stove) that send varying voltages to a voltmeter (the gauge) on the instrument panel. Thus, the sending unit in the fuel tank is in essence a rheostat that is turned higher or lower as a float on the fuel surface rises or falls; and the **fuel gauge** indicates the voltage. An **oil level gauge** (page 58) on the instrument panel indicates the position of a similar float in an oil reservoir off the engine crankcase.

**Fuel-consumption** (or **miles-per-gallon**) gauges on the instrument panel require electronic calculators or mini-computers that divide a *speed* signal (miles per hour) by a *fuel-flow* signal (gallons per hour) and send the result to the gauge. The speed component is provided by the **speedometer,** the primary operational element of which is a magnetized disk or drum that spins at a speed proportional to the rate of turning of the drive shaft. A separate spinning magnet driven by a turbine in a fuel line provides the fuel-flow component. (Fuel flow can be measured by several kinds of apparatus.) An **ETA Meter** on the instrument panel is also operated by a mini-computer: it calculates *estimated time of arrival* from the total-miles setting punched in by the driver, and the total miles driven (from the odometer) since its internal stop-watch was instructed to start keeping time.

## BEHAVIOR PROBLEMS

Any automobile, however new or however well-maintained, will now and then develop noises, odors, vibrations and silences as a result of something not working properly. Any abnormal behavior like this is *telling you something.* Therefore, *pay attention.*

The more common of these ailments are listed in the following pages, together with their possible causes, in order of seriousness. Attached to almost every one is an *urgency rating,* which tells you how important it is that you do something about the problems. No urgency rating means it's not necessary to tell you, such as when your starter won't work; you're not going anywhere until it is repaired.

The range is wide: the air-conditioner can be out of commission for a long time without endangering anyone, but faulty brakes, or a drop in the engine-oil pressure, or serious overheating with clouds of steam need attention NOW.

If there are words you don't understand, look in the index at the back of the book for references that will tell you where to look to find out what they mean.

> ### The Urgency Scale
>
> URGENCY 1: Have the problem investigated next time the car goes to the garage or service station for routine maintenance.
> URGENCY 2: Have the problem investigated the next time you stop for gasoline.
> URGENCY 3: Take the car in as soon as you can conveniently do so.
> URGENCY 4: Take it in today or tomorrow even if it is inconvenient.
> URGENCY 5: Stop at the side of the road immediately.

**Battery runs down when parking overnight or for several days:** The battery is worn out; the switch for the "courtesy lights" (that is, the trunk and glove compartment) does not turn off; an electrical leak in the system.

**Starter won't operate:** The neutral safety switch (in automatic transmission) or the clutch interlock (in manual transmission) is out of adjustment; battery undercharged or worn out; corroded connections at battery posts or other ends of battery cables; failure of the ignition switch, the solenoid switch, or the starter; the fusible link has blown.

**Starter cranks slowly and with difficulty:** URGENCY 4, since the next time it may not crank at all. Battery undercharged or worn out; battery posts or battery ground connection corroded; battery cable damaged; starter solenoid switch beginning to fail.

**Starter goes "ruh-ruh-ruh" but engine doesn't catch:** Out of gasoline; engine flooded by too much pumping on accelerator pedal; wet or deterioriated distributor cap or plug cables;

distributor points out of adjustment; automatic choke needs adjusting; gasoline has water in it; fuel-injection system (gasoline or diesel) malfunctioning; glow plugs malfunctioning (diesel); more complex problems in either ignition system or fuel system may be responsible.

**Engine catches but only after prolonged cranking:** URGENCY 1-4, depending on how exasperating it is. Engine flooded by too much pumping on accelerator pedal; automatic choke or distributor points need adjusting; spark plugs need re-gapping or replacing; more complex problems in either the ignition system or the fuel system may be responsible.

**Engine particularly hard to start when hot:** If starter cranks slowly or balks: bad battery cable connections (URGENCY 3). If the engine catches, but only after prolonged cranking: flooding due to "percolation" of gasoline (no urgency rating; hold accelerator pedal to floor—but don't pump it!—while cranking.)

**Engine stalls repeatedly during warm-up period:** URGENCY 3 because of traffic hazard. Engine idling speed too low; fuel mixture out of adjustment; chilly, damp weather causing ice to form in the carburetor; gasoline is wrong grade for unseasonable weather; distributor points need adjusting; choke out of adjustment; thermostatic vacuum switch, manifold heat valve, or hot-idle compensator malfunctioning; EGR valve stuck open; vacuum leak at carburetor base; automatic choke needs adjusting.

**Engine runs unsteadily; hesitates and jerks:** URGENCY 3. Faulty spark-plug lead; spark plugs need regapping; distributor points need adjusting; automatic choke stuck in closed or partly-closed position; air filter badly plugged; gasoline has water in it; PCV valve or crankcase ventilation filter plugged; EGR valve malfunctioning; engine valves need overhauling.

**Engine stalls on sharp turns:** URGENCY 3. Carburetor float not adjusted properly.

**Engine dies in mid-flight:** Out of gasoline; fuel filter plugged; fuel pump gone bad; water in gasoline; distributor points need adjusting; ignition coil or condenser or electronic-ignition module gone bad; fusible link blown.

**Engine "diesels"—that is, keeps on running after you shut off the ignition:** URGENCY 3. Idling speed set too high; gasoline of too-low octane rating has been used; charge of carbon-cleaning gasoline additive needed; fuel-cut solenoid malfunctioning.

**Squeal under the hood...**

> **On hard turns:** URGENCY 2. Power steering belt.
> **When you race the engine:** URGENCY 2. Alternator belt.
>
> **When you turn on the air-conditioner:** URGENCY 2. Air-conditioner compressor belt.
>
> **Continuous squeal, howl, or whistle:** URGENCY 4. Low fluid level in power steering unit; water pump going bad; vacuum leak at connection on intake manifold.
>
> **Rhythmic squeak under the hood:** URGENCY 4. Belt needs lubricating; valve train not being lubricated adequately.

**Engine spits back through the carburetor on acceleration:** URGENCY 2. Automatic choke needs adjusting; carburetor acceleration pump malfunctioning; electrical leakage via cracks in distributor cap or spark plug leads fires wrong spark plug; intake valve leaking.

**Oil consumption increases appreciably over a short time:** URGENCY 2. Loose oil filter; valve-cover or oil-pressure sending-switch leak; PCV valve or crankcase-ventilation-filter plugged.

**Engine noises...**

**Chirping sound or rhythmic squeak;** URGENCY 4. Valve train not being lubricated adequately.

**Light peck-peck-peck when engine is cold but goes away as engine warms up;** URGENCY 1. Valve tappets need adjusting; hydraulic valve lifter malfunctioning, perhaps only temporarily; worn fuel-pump drive mechanism.

**Light tick-tick-tick when car is in motion:** URGENCY 1. Stone in tire tread; speedometer cable needs lubricating.

**Clack-clack when engine is running:** URGENCY 4. Oil not reaching valve train; inoperative hydraulic valve lifter; wrist pin bearing going bad.

**Heavy thud-thud-thud when engine is running:** URGENCY 5. Failed main bearing or connecting-rod bearing; broken piston.

**Engine slow to warm up:** URGENCY 2. Thermostat stuck in open position; engine-temperature indicator giving an incorrect signal.

**Engine overheats...**

**Indicator says so;** URGENCY 3. Coolant level too low; car overloaded; slipping fan belt; slipping fan clutch; electric cooling fan sluggish; engine-temp indicator giving an incorrect signal; spark timing or diesel fuel-injection timing too retarded.

**Cloud of steam up front says so:** URGENCY 5. Water-pump belt or electric cooling fan has failed; radiator or heater hose has burst or become disconnected; coolant has frozen.

**Water spot or puddle on garage floor or pavement:** If just forward of right front door, after air-conditioner has been running: a normal effect of air-conditioning operating properly. Otherwise, a leak in the cooling system, hence URGENCY 4.

**Oil spot or puddle on garage floor or pavement:** URGENCY 3, or if puddle is large, URGENCY 4. Leak in transmission-cooler system; transmission oil seal leak; power-steering pump seal leak; leaky rocker-arm-cover gasket, oil-pressure sending switch, or front or rear engine crankshaft oil seal; oil filter not screwed on tightly; leaky differential or transaxle oil seal.

**Oil in radiator coolant:** URGENCY 1. Leak in transmission-cooler system in the radiator; oil-spill into coolant overflow tank; leaky or loose cylinder-head gasket.

**Oil-pressure warning light fails to light when you turn ignition on:** URGENCY 4. Bulb needs replacing.

**Oil-pressure warning light goes on, or stays on, or oil-pressure gauge indicates low engine-oil pressure, when engine is running:** URGENCY 5. Do not run the engine more than a few seconds in defiance of oil-pressure warning; serious engine damage may result.

**"Gen" or "Alt" light fails to light when you turn on the ignition before starting the engine:** URGENCY 3. Indicator bulb needs replacing.

**"Gen" or "Alt" light goes on, or "Charge" or "Battery" gauge indicates DISCHARGE at engine speeds above idling speed:**

URGENCY 4. Alternator drive belt slipping or broken; voltage regulator failure; alternator failure.

**Fuel consumption soars:** URGENCY 3. Leak in fuel tank, or in fuel line, or in fuel pump connections, or in carburetor connection; excessive fuel pump pressure; worn float valve in carburetor; dirty air filter; automatic choke not opening completely; timing out of adjustment; fuel-injection system (gasoline or diesel) needs adjusting; manifold heat valve or early-fuel-evaporation control valve malfunctioning; breaker points need replacing; electronic-ignition module malfunctioning; spark plugs need re-gapping or replacing; brake shoe dragging.

**Fuel odor:** URGENCY 2 to 5, depending on how strong the odor is; and where. (If strong *gasoline* odor in engine compartment, URGENCY 5.) Fuel-tank cap missing or loose; leak in fuel tank, fuel line, fuel pump connections, carburetor connection, or fuel-injection assembly (gasoline or diesel); charcoal canister filter needs replacing.

**Exhaust odor inside car:** URGENCY 4, but DRIVE WITH WINDOWS OPEN TO PROVIDE FRESH AIR! See WARNING ABOUT EXHAUST SYSTEMS, next page. Trunk lid open; major leak in exhaust system.

**Rotten-egg exhaust odor:** URGENCY 1. Dirty air filter; automatic choke not opening completely; idling mixture too rich; excessive fuel pump pressure; worn float valve in carburetor.

**Exhaust roar:** URGENCY 3, but DRIVE WITH WINDOWS OPEN TO PROVIDE FRESH AIR! See WARNING ABOUT EXHAUST SYSTEMS, next page. Major leak in exhaust system.

**Exhaust hiss:** URGENCY 3, but see WARNING ABOUT EXHAUST SYSTEMS, next page. Tailpipe crimped or flattened or partially plugged at outlet end.

**Black exhaust smoke:** URGENCY 1. Automatic choke not opening completely; fuel pump pressure too high; worn float valve
in carburetor; dirty air filter; fuel-injection system (gasoline or
diesel) out of adjustment.

**Blue exhaust smoke;** URGENCY 1. PCV valve plugged; leaky
valve stem seals; worn piston rings; defective vacuum control
on automatic transmission, sucking transmission fluid into intake manifold.

### Warning About Exhaust Systems

Leakage in the exhaust system will not shut down the car, but
it may shut down the occupants. Exhaust gas contains a high concentration of carbon monoxide, which can kill you. Exhaust gas
from a leak in the system can seep into the car, particularly when
the car moves little but the engine continues to run, as in traffic
jams or when stalled because of slippery roads. First symptoms
are drowsiness and headache. IF YOU SMELL EXHAUST, OPEN
THE WINDOWS NO MATTER HOW COLD OR WET OR
UNPLEASANT IT IS OUTSIDE; and have the exhaust system
checked promptly. URGENCY 4.

**Engine runs, but car won't move:** One wheel on ice or snow or
in mud; failure in drive train (clutch, transmission, universal joint,
differential or transaxle assembly, drive axle).

**Engine runs normally, but car moves sluggishly:** URGENCY 4.
Manual transmission: clutch needs adjusting or overhaul.
Automatic transmission: transmission-fluid level low; maladjusted
shift linkage to transmission; faulty transmission vacuum control.

**Metallic whine or grinding sound when car is in motion:** URGEN-
CY 4. Built-in device warns of worn brake linings when brakes
are applied; broken spring permits brake shoe to rub against brake
drum or disc; wheel bearing needs lubricating; automatic
transmission needs servicing.

**Car shudders when clutch is engaged:** URGENCY 3. Clutch needs adjusting; loose or broken engine mount; clutch overhaul needed.

**Car vibrates:** URGENCY 3. Unbalanced wheels or tires; worn shock absorbers; incorrect tire pressure in front; tire bulge (flaw); loose lug nuts; worn steering linkages; loose or broken engine mounts; worn or maladjusted bearings; bent wheel; worn universal joints; damaged drive shaft.

**Shift lever jumps out of gear or sticks in gear (manual transmission):** URGENCY 3. Clutch needs adjusting; transmission oil level too low; worn transmission parts.

**Rubbing noise when clutch pedal is pushed in:** URGENCY 2. Bent clutch pedal rubbing on floorboard; clutch linkage needs lubricating; clutch release bearing needs lubricating.

**Gear clash when you shift gears (manual transmission):** URGENCY 3. Clutch needs adjusting; transmission oil level low; worn transmission parts.

**Transmission whines or groans:** URGENCY 4. Transmission-fluid (automatic transmission) or transmission-oil (manual transmission) level too low; plugged transmission-fluid filter.

**CLUNK sound when you reverse direction (automatic transmission):** URGENCY 1. Idling speed too high; differential lubrication level too low; worn universal joint.

**Sluggish shifting from "Park" or "Neutral" to "Reverse" (automatic transmission):** URGENCY 4. Transmission fluid level low; transmission bands or clutches need adjusting; transmission filter needs replacing.

**Sharp metallic rattle or CLUNK on bumps:** URGENCY 1-4, depending on how alarming the sound. Loose shock-absorber mounting; loose or broken exhaust system hanger; worn suspension joints; broken leaf spring.

**Car "hits bottom" on bumps:** URGENCY 2-4, depending on how suddenly the problem has developed. Worn-out shock absorbers; broken leaf spring.

**Brake pedal travels abnormally far before the brakes work:** First: put car in reverse, slowly, and brake to a stop; do this two or three times, and more if it seems to be solving the problem. If it doesn't then URGENCY 4, and *drive carefully!* System needs brake fluid, or front or rear brakes need adjusting or overhauling.

**Brake pedal sinks all the way to the floor:** URGENCY 4. *Drive very slowly and carefully* to home and mechanic, and be prepared to use your parking brake instead of, or in addition to, the foot brake. The symptom indicates that both brake systems have failed.

**Brake-pedal travel increases on long downgrade:** This is known as "fading:" result of drum brakes being too hot. Shift to lower gear to hold speed down and give the brakes a rest.

**Brake pedal feels spongy:** URGENCY 4. Brake-fluid level is low and air has been sucked into the brake system. *Drive very carefully until the problem is corrected.*

**Brakes don't respond fully to brake pedal:** If brakes are very wet (if you have driven through deep water or puddles), dry them out by holding brake pedal down while driving a few hundred feet. If this doesn't clear up the problem, then URGENCY 4 and *drive slowly and carefully.* Be prepared to use your parking brake instead of, or in addition to, the foot brake. Vacuum booster failed (power brake); obstruction interfering with brake-pedal travel.

**Power brake loses power immediately when engine stalls:** URGENCY 4. Inoperative check valve in power brake system.

**Brake pedal pulsates when depressed slightly:** URGENCY 1. Brake drum out-of-round or brake disc warped; pair of radial tires badly matched.

**Brakes squeal or chatter or make scratching sound:** URGENCY 1. Mud has splashed into brake assembly on wheel (temporary effect); linings need replacing (automatic warning built into brake linings); brakes have been relined with hard-composition "long-life" linings.

**Car pulls to one side when you brake:** URGENCY 4, and *drive slowly and carefully:* Soft front tire; one brake lining wet or both brake linings on one side of car; brake fluid or grease in brake lining on one wheel; brake linings need replacing.

**Brakes grab (that is, seize suddenly):** NORMAL if it happens only when brakes are cold, especially power brakes. Otherwise, URGENCY 4. Brake fluid or grease on brake linings.

**Brakes drag (that is, car doesn't coast freely):** If parking brake has been fully released, then URGENCY 4. Broken brake-return spring.

**Excessive play in steering wheel before car responds:** URGENCY 1. Steering box needs adjusting; steering system joints need replacing.

**Whine or screech when steering wheel is turned sharply:** URGENCY 3. Loose or glazed power-steering belt; worn power-steering pump; worn steering box.

**Hard steering:** URGENCY 4. Front tires underinflated (manual steering); steering gearbox needs oil (manual steering); pump belt broken (power steering); power-steering fluid level low (usually accompanied by hissing sound.)

**Car wanders or darts to right or left:** URGENCY 4 if trouble has developed suddenly; otherwise URGENCY 1-3, depending on how unstable the car feels. One front tire underinflated; radial tires need switching; loose lug nuts; loose or worn front-wheel bearing; front end needs aligning or overhauling; steering gear box needs adjusting; front shock absorbers need replacing; stabilizer bar mountings need replacing.

**Front-wheel shimmy:** URGENCY 4 if trouble developed suddenly; otherwise URGENCY 3. Loose lug nuts; mud accumulation in front wheel (front-wheel-drive car); underflated front tire; un- balanced wheel-tire combinations; out-of-round tire; radial tires need rotating or switching; loose or worn front-wheel bearing; weak shock absorber; front end needs aligning; broken or loose engine mount; worn steering-system joints.

**Tires wear unevenly:** URGENCY 1. Underinflation; tire needs balancing; bent wheel; weak shock absorber; front end needs aligning.

**Acrid odor of overheated electrical equipment:** URGENCY 5. With engine off and lights off, check for smoke under the hood. If none, turn lights on; and if no smoke, then URGENCY 4. Switch inside car or under hood needs replacing; accessory motor needs replacing.

**Wrong light turns on:** URGENCY 1. Light socket somewhere in the malfunctioning system is poorly grounded.

**Light bulbs burn out prematurely:** URGENCY 1. Voltage regulator set for too-high voltage.

**Headlight brightness fluctuates rapidly and markedly ("flutters"):** URGENCY 4. Short-circuit in headlight system activating circuit breakers in the system; loose connection in headlight circuit.

**Headlights brighten with increasing engine speed ("headlight flare"):** URGENCY 1. Worn-out battery; faulty voltage regulator.

**Turn-signal lights flash at wrong speed:** URGENCY 3. Burned-out turn-signal bulb; faulty stop-light bulb permits current leakage; turn-signal flasher unit needs replacing.

**Heater fails to heat:** URGENCY 3. Blown fuse on heater motor; cooling-system thermostat needs replacing; heater hose plugged; heater core needs flushing; thermostat on heater core malfunctioning.

**Defroster causes windshield fogging:** URGENCY 3. Leak in heater core.

**Air-conditioner fails to cool:** Broken or slipping compressor belt; refrigerant level too low; air-conditioner control system inoperative.

**Windshield washer won't squirt:** Washer solution used up; washer solution frozen; disconnected or leaky washer-solution hose; plugged jets at windshield; valves inside the pump need replacing; pump motor or switch inoperative.

**Horn won't blow:** Wire connector pulled loose from horn relay or from horn; horn needs adjusting; horn relay needs replacing; horn button needs replacing.

**Horn won't stop blowing:** EMERGENCY PROCEDURE: pull wire connector loose from horn. Horn relay or horn button stuck in ON position.

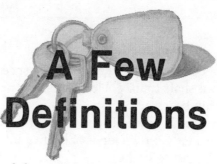

# A Few Definitions

**Axle:** In automobile usage, an axle is a shaft (see page 163) that drives and rotates with a drive wheel—a rear wheel in a rear-wheel-drive car and a front wheel in a front-wheel-drive car.

**Bearing:** Any carefully-sized hole that guides a rotating shaft or rod or wheel so that it will rotate without wobble. Sketch "a" below shows a *sleeve bearing;* the purpose of this bearing is to permit the shaft and the wheel attached to it to rotate. A large number of different kinds of bearings are used in an automobile: wheel bearings, and bearings that permit and guide the rotation of the fan, the alternator, the air-conditioner compressor, to name a few. The windshield-wiper arm swings to and fro on a bearing. The window crank is held in proper position and made to

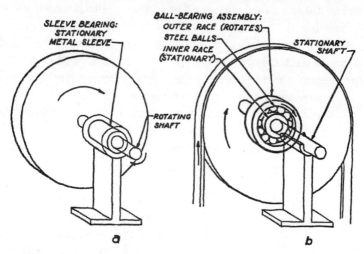

*Two Kinds of Bearings*

turn true by a bearing inside the door. The speedometer needle is attached to a shaft that is held in position and permitted to turn by suitable bearing.

Bearings are usually made of special low-friction wear-resistant materials, particularly certain kinds of bronze and special plastics.

Ball bearings and roller bearings provide lowest friction and maximum service life. In sketch "b," the ball bearing permits the wheel to rotate on a shaft that is held stationary. Roller bearings are generally similar: the steel balls are replaced by short cylinders. The overall effect is the same: the outer doughnut is separated from the inner doughnut by the rollers, and the two doughnuts can rotate relative to one another, with little friction, because the rollers between them roll freely.

**Bushing:** A sleeve bearing that holds and guides a shaft that rotates back and forth rather than around and around. Thus the shaft of a windshield-wiper blade would be said to be mounted in a bushing rather than in a bearing.

**Cable:** In automobile usage, a cable is always further identified: a *spark cable* is a heavily insulated wire that conducts current from the distributor to a spark plug; *battery cables* are insulated thick wires that carry heavy currents from the battery to the starter solenoid and to ground; the *brake cable* is a steel connecting link between the parking-brake lever or pedal and the rear brakes; the *speedometer cable* transmits the rotational speed of the automobile wheels, via the drive shaft, to the speedometer, so that the speedometer can indicate both speed and distance traveled.

**Cam:** The next sketch shows what a cam is and "c" on page 165 shows how it works to cause the valves in an automobile engine to open and close. As the camshaft turns, the cam forces a pushrod upward and thus forces the rocker arm to rock, and the rocker arm in turn forces the engine valve to open against the resistance of the valve spring.

More generally, a cam is a disk of non-uniform diameter mounted on a shaft in such a manner that a pushrod or other "cam follower" riding on its periphery is caused to rise and fall as the shaft and disk rotate (or move or swing in and out if the shaft is vertical). Thus, a cam may be a circular disk mounted off-center on a shaft. It may also be a square disk with the shaft running through its center. This is the kind of cam that is used in the distributor of a four-cylinder engine: with each revolution of the camshaft, an arm that presses against the periphery of the cam swings in and out four times. In an eight-cylinder engine, the disk mounted on the shaft is octagonal in shape, so the cam follower swings in and out eight times for each revolution of the camshaft.

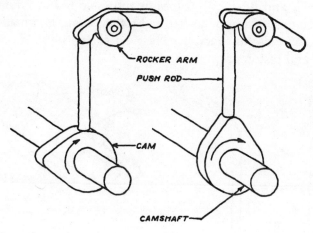

*Cam*

**Circuit:** In an automobile, the word means electrical circuits exclusively. Generally speaking, such a circuit is an electrical path from one post of a battery to the other, by way of some apparatus, such as an electric motor or a light bulb. For example, if an electric motor is placed in the path from one battery post to the other, then the electric current will flow through the motor and cause it to run.

Most electrical circuits in an automobile make use of the steel engine block, or the frame, or the body, or some other structural member which is capable of conducting electric current. Thus, if a wire connects one post of the battery to a light bulb, a second wire connects the light bulb with the frame of the car, and a third wire connects the frame of the car with the other post of the battery, then these elements together will constitute an electrical circuit. Any electrical connection to the frame, body, or engine is called a *ground* connection.

**Cylinder and piston:** Categorically, any hole occupied by a movable plug that fits the hole reasonably snugly is a cylinder-and-piston assembly. In practice, one or both ends of the hole are capped, and fitted with pipes or tubes, so that a liquid or gas can be pushed out or sucked in by the piston, and made to perform some useful function. The next sketch illustrates two cylinder-and-piston assemblies.

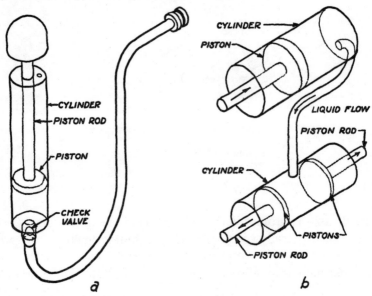

*Two Cylinder-and-Piston Assemblies*

In a simple bicycle pump, a check valve at the bottom of the cylinder prevents air from being sucked into the cylinder via the hose when the handle and the attached piston are pulled up, and so air flows around the piston (a simple leather cup) instead. When you push down on the handle, the leather cup resists leakage of air but the check valve does not: the ball drops downward, out of the hold it has been plugging, and permits air to flow freely through the hose.

The assembly shown in "b" illustrates how mechanical force may be transmitted hydraulically. If the upper cylinder is filled with oil, force on the piston rod will cause the piston to move into the upper cylinder and this will force oil into the lower cylinder. This flow will result in the pistons and piston rods of the lower cylinder being forced outward. Thus, mechanical force applied to the upper piston rod will cause the lower piston rods to exert mechanical force in their turn. Contrarily, of the piston in the upper cylinder is pulled outward, oil will be sucked from the lower piston into the upper one, and in consequence, the pistons in the lower cylinder will be pulled inward.

There are many different cylinder-and-piston assemblies in an automobile. The brake system employs inter-connected cylinders similar to the combination shown in the previous sketch ("b"). The basic operation of an internal-combustion engine depends upon a cylinder-and-piston assembly. The acceleration pump on the carburetor, the power-steering mechanism, the vacuum booster used on power brakes, the shock absorbers—each of these has a cylinder-and-piston assembly at its heart.

**Gasket:** A layer of paper, or cardboard, or asbestos, or plastic, or rubber, or soft metal such as copper or brass, that is placed between two metal surfaces to absorb imperfections in their surfaces and prevent the leakage of liquid or gas at the joint.

**Gear:** A toothed wheel, shown on page 112. Few gears in an automobile are as simple as the ones portrayed; the shapes of gear teeth are ordinarily much more sophisticated than those in the sketch, to reduce the noise of gear contact, and to spread wear of the gear teeth over wider areas of contact.

**Grease vs. oil:** Grease is oil to which thickener has been added to give it greater body and to prevent its flowing away from the spot where it is needed. Both oil and grease are used for lubricating joints, gears, bearings, and other points of contact where surfaces would wear if they were not covered with a film of oil. The lubricating liquid used in an engine crankcase is invariably called *oil;* the lubricant that is squirted into steering-system and suspension-system joints is invariably called *grease.* In between there are borderline cases: the lubricant in the differential, for example, may be called either oil or grease, and so may the lubricant in manual transmissions. (Automatic-transmission *fluid* serves a lubricating function, but it is not primarily a lubricant; it is never called either "oil" or "grease.")

**Hydraulic system:** A closed system designed to transmit force or motion by causing a liquid to flow from one cylinder to another. The principle is illustrated in the "b" sketch on page 160.

**Linkage:** A rod or lever, or a combination of rods and levers, with appropriate ends for fastening to other components. Thus, the *clutch linkage* is the array of levers and pushrods that transmits motion of the clutch pedal to the clutch plate, and the *steering linkage* is the collection of levers and pushrods that transmits the motion of the pitman arm of a steering system to the front wheels. The mechanism that redirects the hot air when you move a "defroster" lever on the instrument panel is called a linkage, and so is the mechanism that causes the windshield wipers to operate when you move a lever or turn a knob on the instrument panel.

**Seal:** A doughnut of soft material that prevents leakage of air, oil, water, or refrigerant around a shaft. Thus a seal around the shaft of the water pump prevents coolant from leaking around the shaft where it passes through the outer wall of the pump. Similar seals prevent the leakage of oil around the crankshaft where it goes through the front and rear walls of the crankcase, and around the transmission shafts where they go through the front and rear walls of the transmission case, and so on.

**Sending unit:** A component of an instrument system that provides the electrical impulses to activate the other component. An example: a sending unit located in the gasoline tank delivers electrical voltage to the gauge on the instrument panel in an amount in proportion to the level of gasoline in the tank. Similarly, a sending unit that is located in an appropriate part of the engine-lubrication system provides electrical voltage (in proportion to the magnitude of the oil pressure) to the gauge or alarm light on the instrument panel.

**Shaft:** A cylindrical bar, usually of steel, that supports rotating items such as wheels, pulleys, flywheels, etc., or transmits power or motion by rotation. There are dozens of shafts of various kinds in an automobile. The *steering column* imparts the rotation of the steering wheel to the gearbox. The pivot that the brake pedal swings on is a shaft: the motion of the pedal there is not a complete rotation, but it is nevertheless a rotary motion. The water pump and fan operate on the same shaft; and the alternator and the starter are built around main shafts that transmit power from an electrical source to a mechanical load or vice-versa. The crankshaft is perhaps the most important shaft in the automobile: this is the shaft the flywheel rotates on, the U-shaped "crank" sections interrupt the straight line of the shaft, but it both supports rotating items and transmits power by its own rotation.

**Solenoid:** A particular kind of coil of electric wire that generates a magnetic field inside the coil when current passes through the wire. In most applications in an automobile, the magnetic field is harnessed to an electric switch, so that when the current flows through the coil or wire an electromagnet causes the electric switch to be turned on or off. The *starter solenoid* operates the heavy-duty switch that supplies current to the starter; in addition, in most cars, the solenoid also operates a linkage that engages the starter drive gear with the engine flywheel and causes the flywheel to rotate and the engine to start.

**Vacuum:** A more common word is "suction." The cylinders of a gasoline engine generate a vacuum because within each cylinder the piston, moving downward with the exhaust valve closed, sucks air into the cylinder.

**Valve:** A device for controlling the flow of liquid or gas through an opening. The water faucet is a familiar example: by turning the wheel, knob, or lever, you permit or prevent the flow of water and control its rate of flow, and if the valve is faulty, the water will drip instead of stopping when you turn off the valve. There is a similar "screw valve" at the bottom of an automobile radiator so that the coolant can be drained from the cooling system. There are many types of valves in an automobile. Most basic is the engine valve, shown in the next sketch ("c"): a mushroom-shaped object with a beveled edge that rides up and down; when it is tightly closed it seals an opening called a *valve port* and prevents the flow of gasoline-air mixture through the port. Sketch "b" shows a *butterfly*, or *damper*, valve: a flat plate of substantially the same diameter as the pipe it is mounted in; when it is turned crosswise, it blocks the pipe completely; when it is turned longitudinally, it permits almost unrestricted flow through the pipe; and it throttles the flow through the pipe when it is in the various positions between the two extremes. The butterfly valve is crucial to the carburetor, and it is used to direct the flow of air in the heater-defroster-air-conditioner system. The *check valve* (sketch "a" on page 160) is useful throughout an automobile: the fuel pump depends upon a pair of check valves that permit gasoline to be sucked from the gasoline tank on an upward stroke of the pump diaphragm, and then to flow out to the carburetor on the downward stroke. The carburetor, the shock absorbers, and the windshield-washer pump all require check valves of one kind or another.

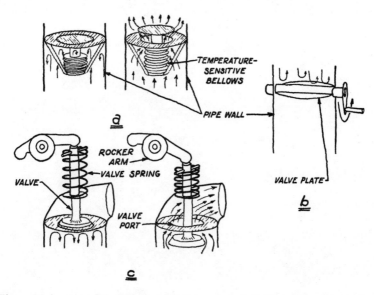

*Three Valves: a) Thermostat Valve, closed (left) and open (right); b) Butterfly Valve (closed); c) Engine Valve, closed (left) and open (right).*

The *thermostat valve* is actuated by the temperature of the fluid it controls. A thermostat valve is shown in sketch "a" above, in both the open and closed position. A thermostat in the cooling system prevents the circulation of coolant when the engine—and the coolant—are cold, but permits the coolant to circulate after the engine warms up. This is accomplished by placing a temperature-sensitive bellows in the coolant that will warm up as the engine warms up. As the coolant and the bellows get warmer, the bellows expands and pushes the valve stem upward, opening the valve port and allowing the coolant to circulate through the cooling system.

# INDEX